LIFE IN GEORGIAN RICHMOND, NORTH YORKSHIRE

'... it is this delightful habit of journalising which largely
contributes to form the easy style of writing for which ladies are
so generally celebrated.'
Jane Austen.

LIFE IN GEORGIAN RICHMOND, NORTH YORKSHIRE

A DIARY AND ITS SECRETS

**Jane Hatcher and
Bob Woodings**

PEN & SWORD
HISTORY

AN IMPRINT OF PEN & SWORD BOOKS LTD.
YORKSHIRE - PHILADELPHIA

First published in Great Britain in 2018 by
PEN & SWORD HISTORY
An imprint of
Pen & Sword Books Ltd
Yorkshire - Philadelphia

ISBN: 9781526707383

Typeset by SRJ Info Jnana System Pvt Ltd.

Printed and bound in England By CPI Group (UK) Ltd, Croydon, CR0 4YY

Pen & Sword Books Ltd incorporates the Imprints of Aviation, Atlas,
Family History, Fiction, Maritime, Military, Discovery, Politics, History,
Archaeology, Select, Wharncliffe Local History, Wharncliffe True Crime,
Military Classics, Wharncliffe Transport, Leo Cooper, The Praetorian Press,
Remember When, Seaforth Publishing and Frontline Publishing.

For a complete list of Pen & Sword titles please contact

PEN & SWORD BOOKS LTD
47 Church Street, Barnsley, South Yorkshire, S70 2AS, England
E-mail: enquiries@pen-and-sword.co.uk
Website: www.pen-and-sword.co.uk

or

PEN AND SWORD BOOKS
1950 Lawrence Rd, Havertown, PA 19083, USA
E-mail: Uspen-and-sword@casematepublishers.com
Website: www.penandswordbooks.com

Front cover illustration credits

Samuel and Nathaniel Buck, *The South-west Prospect of Richmond in the
County of York* (WA.Suth.L.4.35).
Image copyright of Ashmolean Museum, University of Oxford

and

Gillray cartoon of Militia Soldiers, reproduced courtesy of the North
Yorkshire County Record Office

Contents

Foreword

Life in Georgian Richmond, North Yorkshire presents those who study the Georgian period with a unique source of material, based on a diary from the mid-1760s, which we affectionately call 'The Richmond Diary'. This hitherto unknown historical document revealingly conveys what it actually felt like to be alive then. Not only are the details of daily life – and almost daily death – there, but also information on medical treatments, how letters were sent between different parts of the country, how much travel took place between London and the provinces, and even what gardening was done. Most of all, for social historians, here is precise material on many fashionable leisure activities, including assemblies, horse racing, polite conversation and, most frequently, taking tea.

Family historians can glimpse a rare insight into how their ancestors lived day by day. How did a woman, perhaps not very well off, look for a husband? Or a widow, in declining health, have to stand back while the next generation took over running the household. How important were ribbons to young Georgian women? Your male ancestor might have been one of the soldiers marching south from Scotland to London through the pages of the diary, or perhaps more likely, a militia man undergoing annual training.

Have you been fortunate enough to inherit a portrait of a Georgian ancestor and wondered how it came to be painted? Our Diarist recounts that process, looking on perhaps a little enviously as some friends had their portraits 'taken' – yes, we learn to speak the language of the day.

Read on – we invite you to enter the world of our Diarist!

JH and BW

Yorkshire, 2017

Illustrations

Preliminaries

Secrets of 'The Richmond Diary'

It rarely happens, a hitherto unknown historical document, of immense importance, just turning up. But in 1988 it did. A daily diary, running from mid-1764 to early 1766, and one that is so unusual for this date, we have called it 'The Richmond Diary', and referred to it as such throughout this book. The document 'The Richmond Diary' was kept by an unknown woman, living in Richmond, North Yorkshire, not only setting down what she did, day by day, but also trying to understand herself and those around her, and her place in the world, now and in the future.

Of course many historians have known all about this Georgian world, and some have written about it. But now we can all benefit from this remarkable source, a first-person account of what that world was like, and the feelings that accompanied that life. The more the authors have studied this diary, the more revealing it has become. For example, it can be read as an informative feminist document, recording how women organise their time so that they can regularly meet together, and how different age groups emerge.

Who is this anonymous Diarist? How old is she? Is she unmarried, a mother, a widow? Where does she live? What is her background, that she is as literate as 'The Richmond Diary' suggests? The authors have attempted to unravel the mystery, identifying the circle of relatives, friends and acquaintances, that flit across those daily entries like the cast of a play, or characters in the novels that the Diarist obviously enjoyed reading. These figures are a fascinating mix of individuals, old and young, rich and poor, living in and outside Richmond. What did the Diarist know of them? What did she see behind their behaviour? They belong not only to Richmond, but also to several North Yorkshire and Teesdale villages, and even to London. Family historians will find it well worth their while to look in our careful index to see if the person they seek can be found here.

At the very beginning of 'The Richmond Diary', the writer introduces it as 'The Journal Continued', implying that it is the second volume she has so compiled. If only the first had not disappeared! As Catherine Morland, the heroine of Jane Austen's early novel, *Northanger Abbey,* is lectured: 'Not keep a journal! How are your absent cousins to understand the tenor of your life … without one? How are the civilities and compliments of every day to be related as they ought to be, unless noted down every evening in a journal?' This was written only some thirty years after 'The Richmond Diary'.

Structure of *Life in Georgian Richmond, North Yorkshire*

To help family and social historians who may not be familiar with all aspects of the Georgian period, in *Life in Georgian Richmond* the authors have attempted to provide contexts for 'The Richmond Diary'. Some general background material on the mid-1760s is followed by more incisive extrapolations drawn from the document itself. Pen portraits of the family and friends of the Diarist have been compiled following many readings and re-readings of the entries, and by researching the people using a wide range of sources. It is only after this process that an attempt can be made to identify who the diarist may be.

The main locations featured in 'The Richmond Diary' are introduced under 'Towns and Locations', followed by studies of a number of topics relating to the mid-1760s as evidenced by the manuscript. Lastly, but most important of all, comes the precise text of 'The Richmond Diary', transcribed precisely as it was written in the mid-1760s. Interspersed with its entries, and clearly differentiated from them in the text, is a commentary providing background information and interpretation.

Approaching 'The Richmond Diary'

The Diarist is fascinated by the world in which she lives – almost like a twenty-first century anthropologist. Like Jane Austen, she is seeking to document and analyse in her pages just what is taking place around her. She obviously recognises the identity of her cast of characters, and to a degree understands what they are up to, where they have come from, what they are doing, and perhaps what is likely to be their future. Her ambition and achievement in recording this is quite remarkable. The authors of *Life in Georgian Richmond, North Yorkshire* have attempted to look behind the words of 'The Richmond Diary' to provide a window through which readers can see the Diarist's daily life.

'The Richmond Diary' is distinctive in inviting the reader to enter into and experience the world of this intelligent and literate woman living in Georgian England's traditional patriarchal society. But our Diarist's world is emerging from this patriarchy, she shows how her generation has different concerns and ambitions from those of her mother's generation. Remarkably, she even details for us the development of a school for young ladies, recruiting its students from well beyond Richmond, and preparing them for the new and emerging opportunities.

The characters in 'The Richmond Diary' cannot be separated from what occupies their time, where they find their amusements, how they spend their days. The Diarist is exceptional in providing detailed information, whether of taking tea, letter writing or shopping. She goes to dances, to see plays, to visit friends, to walk to the shops, to run her household, to see the races, to gather news from London. What brings alive the Diarist's Georgian world is explored under the heading 'The Richmond Diary and the 1760s'.

She observes and records an unexpected sense of how her friends and other Richmond residents actually behave, and perceives aspects of their morality. Money plays such a part in this world, in its authority and dealings, which can betray and deceive, and change the status of a generation. It would seem that the Diarist, through her family background knows this all too well. What does her income amount to, and what are her financial obligations? This, as the Diary illustrates was a period of entrepreneurship, when more people were trying to earn money to spend on an increasing number of consumable items, including fashionable clothes.

Format of 'The Richmond Diary'

The fifty-six pages of 'The Richmond Diary' contain 480 daily entries from 24 July 1764 to 16 January 1766, the only break being two months at the end of 1764 when the Diarist goes to stay with relatives. That the document relates to the Yorkshire Richmond, then a very fashionable town, is not in doubt. The precise identification of the Diarist is more difficult as the manuscript has little autobiographical content. She does not give names to herself or her closest relatives, but fortunately provides links to the Emersons of Winston, near Barnard Castle in County Durham, and the Smiths of Easby just outside Richmond.

The gender is clear; the writer is a 'she' as the content is entirely feminine. She has male dancing partners, orders stays and petticoats, and trails the shops searching for ribbons. She is clearly single, and almost certainly has not been married, as there is no hint that she was a widow.

The diary entries are exceptionally neat, written on paper which has been carefully lined in faint pencil. The Diarist has clear and legible handwriting, although the ink has faded. Daily entries follow a consistent pattern. Each page starts with the full date, including the day of the week, month and number in the month. All subsequent entries follow a similar pattern.

The entries are more consistent in spelling than are found in the texts of many eighteenth-century writers. There are very few erasures, indicating that the author has in all probability copied out her journal, as she intended it to be read, from original notes. She is not only well-educated, but where we know words have been misspelt, they are usually an attempt to write phonetically what has been mentioned that day but was outside the author's full understanding. She carefully uses very specifically appropriate forms of address, for the eldest of her cousins, and for the various Mr Allens. We learn some contemporary usages, such as going 'down street' for going to the shops, and the old word 'thust' for 'just' as in 'recently'.

Most entries start with a note of the weather. If news has been received from people living away, this follows. Next comes an account of various social activities, sometimes including what must have been the main topic of conversation that day, and lastly what had happened to other people – occasionally childbirth and weddings, but most often deaths and funerals. Health is mentioned only if it has had an adverse impact on the Diarist's ability to follow her normal activities. Expenditure is erratically included, but this diary was not an account book.

'The Richmond Diary' was clearly intended as a record for posterity of the author's life and times. This record is largely dispassionate, and it may be that there was something of a hidden agenda in the observations carefully made. As the essays that follow under the heading of 'Contexts' make clear, this was a period of immense social and economic change, both nationally and locally.

Contexts

Georgian Background to *Life in Georgian Richmond*

'The Richmond Diary' provides a valuable insight into how a provincial town saw the mid-1760s, an exciting time for the nation. A new king, George III, was only a few years into his reign. He was a young man, only in his mid-20s when the diary begins, and the first of the Hanoverian monarchs to have been born in London, not Germany. He succeeded his grandfather, George II, in 1760, because his father, Frederick Lewis, Prince of Wales, had died young in 1751. The much younger Princess of Wales, Augusta, lived on at Kew as a dowager until 1772, so was present in the background of the diary.

George III had, soon after becoming king, in 1761 married Queen Charlotte, and they were to produce fifteen children, including nine sons, the eldest becoming the next king (George IV), the 3rd son the one after that (William IV), and another producing a daughter who became Queen Victoria. Thus the contribution of the diary's young king to national history was to be immense. The Diarist's circle had a link to the royal court through her relative-by-marriage William Allen, thus news of the family and the infant children, as yet few in number, is likely to have been known in Richmond, although discreetly not conveyed to the diary.

George III, our longest reigning king, tends to be remembered for his later sad years battling illness, and to have been on the throne when the American colonies were lost, but his earlier life, which coincided with the diary, was very different. Known for his frugal home life, in contrast to the extravagant lifestyle of his successor, he was a cultured man in whose time the arts flourished, and he would, only a couple of years after the diary concludes, support the foundation of the Royal Academy of Art in 1768. The nation's burgeoning interest in the arts is well represented in the diary.

Recent research has brought to light just how enthusiastic a collector of paintings George III was. In just one year, 1762, he acquired a large number of Italian works from the British Consul in

Venice, Joseph Smith, including pictures by Canaletto, Sebastiano and Marco Ricci, and Zuccarelli. It was already known that many of the large country seats around Richmond, including Aske Hall, Raby Castle and Hornby Castle, had fine collections of works of art, but 'The Richmond Diary' explicitly demonstrates that an interest in acquiring pictures was being taken by people in the Diarist's relatively modest circle. Two of her closest friends have their portraits painted by the artist Henry Pickering, well known in the north of England for such works. That he took a showroom in Richmond to display his work is an important new detail of how such artists operated. On her return from staying with her relatives in Winston over one Christmas period, the Diarist also delivered for them a picture to the Yorke family, who were known to support the arts and would later host the Richmond 'Athenaeum' at their mansion on The Green.

The king was familiar with the fashionable developments in music at the time. His father, Frederick, a keen cello player, had commissioned Arne's 'Rule Britannia', and reference is made elsewhere to the surprising coincidence that the period of the diary covers almost exactly the time of the young Mozart's sojourn in London. Mozart was befriended while in London by Johann Christian Bach, the 11th and youngest son of Johann Sebastian, who had been invited to London in 1762 to compose for the King's Theatre. The Diarist's circle's interest in music is covered in the section on her social activities. Furthermore, she provides some of the most revealing information on the activities of troupes of players in the provinces yet discovered, an apt association for a document set in the town which still has its famous Georgian Theatre Royal.

Most important of all is the architectural background which links Richmond with the national scene. George III was particularly knowledgeable about the many styles of architecture then fashionable, having been tutored in his youth by the great architect Sir William Chambers, a Scotsman who had been educated at Ripon, not far from Richmond. Chambers, along with his possibly more famous fellow Scotsman Robert Adam, had been appointed to the Office of Works in 1761. Great works of architecture were arising all over the country, and the Richmond area was no exception.

All around Richmond at the time the diary was being written, fine architectural compositions were being created, particularly those designed by the prolific York-based architect, John Carr. At Constable Burton in Wensleydale, between 1762 and 1768, he created a classical villa in the Palladian style fine enough to be included in *Vitruvius Britannicus*, a series of books which defined great architecture in the eighteenth century. Nearer to Richmond, between 1765 and 1769, Carr made classical additions and modifications to Aske Hall for Sir Lawrence Dundas, designed a remodelling of Clints Hall near Marske in Swaledale 1762–3 (since demolished), and carried out major works at Hornby Castle near Catterick 1760–70 (now also largely lost).

In the town itself, many older houses were being rebuilt as handsome Georgian town houses, such as that of the Diarist's friend Dr James Pringle, whose house in Newbiggin was brand new. Also in Newbiggin, she might have been somewhat surprised by the appearance of another new town house, that built by the brother-in-law of her close friend Mrs Wilson, Leonard Raw, which had been built in a style more familiar in Gothick follies. The Diarist would have been familiar with the nearby Cumberland Temple (now known as Culloden Tower), a particularly handsome and elaborate Gothick folly belonging to the Yorke family, whose landscaped grounds she often visited.

The appreciation of both natural and man-made landscapes was a key aspect of Georgian culture. Fashionable artists posed families in such settings, and might even show them playing musical instruments, as in Johann Christian Fiedler's 'Concert near Darmstadt'. The enjoyment of music in a bucolic setting was behind the concept of Georgian pleasure gardens, such as the famous Vauxhall Gardens in London, where Hook's ballad 'Sweet Lass of Richmond Hill' was to become such a hit. Richmond had its own smaller pleasure garden, called Placendale (probably a corruption of Pleasing Dale), behind the King's Head Hotel, as well as the Yorke family's landscaped grounds, a 'must see' for Georgian visitors to Richmond.

A handsome Georgian structure of more utilitarian purpose which clearly played an important part in the Diarist's life in Richmond was the fine bridge designed by the leading architect Sir Thomas Robinson near Winston. Its completion, shortly before 'The Richmond Diary' begins, must have influenced her decision to live in Richmond while maintaining close contact with her relatives at Winston.

Of course there was another, more disorderly, side to the image of culture and elegance perpetuated about Georgian times. Doubtless during the period covered by 'The Richmond Diary' there were thefts and assaults taking place in the town, resulting in court appearances, but the Diarist is either unaware of these or chooses not to record them. The only court case she mentions is on 10 October 1765, when the unfortunate Miss Wrather, a haberdasher, had to appear before the Borough Quarter Sessions 'for having a lottery', presumably without proper authority. Richmond was unusual in having its own Quarter Sessions, in addition to those held in the North Riding of Yorkshire.

There was, of course, also poverty, which ecclesiastical parishes were expected to alleviate. Richmond had a 'poorhouse' in Frenchgate, on the east side just above the parish church, which took in those unable to look after themselves for reasons of chronic illness, mental incapacity as well as poverty. A series of poor harvests and resulting high grain prices caused great distress in the Yorkshire Dales in the 1750s. In 1756 the mayor of Richmond raised a subscription from the better-off townsfolk to purchase corn to sell on to the poor inhabitants at a reasonable price. Residents elsewhere in the vicinity, however, reacted in a manner which, although taking place before 'The Richmond Diary' begins, was to have a profound influence on a topic appearing frequently in its pages.

On 3 December 1757, a group of working men in Wensleydale, including miners, masons and knitters, having protested violently in Askrigg against the price of corn, decided to march to Richmond, the most significant administrative centre in Richmondshire, where they hoped to find a solution to their grievance.

Fearing that the town would suffer damage, possibly by burning, the Mayor, apothecary Christopher Wayne, read the Riot Act in the Market Place. As the mob did not then disperse as required, the ringleaders were committed to prison in the gaol in Newbiggin. County magistrates Christopher Crowe of Kiplin, and William Turner who owned Clints near Marske in Swaledale, promised to lead the defence of the inhabitants. A couple of days later, hearing that the rebels were reassembling in Askrigg with the intention of marching to Richmond to release the prisoners, magistrates Crowe and Sir Ralph Milbanke set off with a large number – said to be 700 – of local gentlemen on horses, and other townsfolk – perhaps 200 – on foot. Hearing that the Askrigg mob had dispersed, they turned back, but rioting erupted again a few days later, and on 8 December another armed group, this time led by William Allen, the Diarist's relative by marriage, rode out to Wensleydale. They brought back with them the thirteen ringleaders who had surrendered to them.

William Allen wrote it up in a diary, which has since disappeared but was seen early in the nineteenth century by the Richmond historian Christopher Clarkson, who summarised the various consequences of the event. Among these was that Christopher Crowe was granted the Freedom of the Borough early in 1758 by the grateful Richmond authorities. When the Richmondshire Militia was embodied on 13 July 1759, it was under the command of Sir Ralph Milbanke as Colonel, and with William Allen and Christopher Crowe as Majors.

Other serious outbreaks of disorder did, of course, occur elsewhere. Less than a month after its embodiment, the Richmondshire Militia was required to march north to Northumberland to deal with a rebellion of pitmen refusing to comply with the requirement of the Militia Act to serve as militiamen. The rebellion was put down without the loss of a single Richmondshire soldier.

The presence of the Militia is of course noted regularly in 'The Richmond Diary'. Military history of a more general nature is brought to us in its pages when three companies of foot soldiers, being marched south from Scotland to London, pass through Richmond in February 1765. Serious outbreaks of disorder were to occur in Swaledale during the Beldi Hill Dispute, involving the Diarist's uncle, Thomas Smith, but this was shortly after 'The Richmond Diary' ends, so of course there is no reference to these.

National events are rarely mentioned specifically, notable exceptions being the deaths of members of the royal family, the old Duke of Cumberland on 31 October 1765, and the king's youngest brother, Frederick William, on 29 December 1765. Evidence of how the subsequent periods of official mourning were dealt with provincially is provided by 'The Richmond Diary'.

'The Richmond Diary' as Georgian Local History

Local history inevitably reflects national trends, and 'The Richmond Diary' provides a vivid insight into many of the social and economic transitions which the country was undergoing in the mid-1760s. Much of *Life in Georgian Richmond, North Yorkshire* focuses on social changes, but economic undercurrents are also well documented. The nascent 'Industrial Revolution' is there in the diary pages, such as the Diarist's purchase of coal, then a fuel increasingly being used in domestic hearths. Early coalmines worked around Etherley, west of Bishop Auckland, where the seams were fairly near the surface and could be accessed by shallow bell-pits, saw Richmond benefiting from coal cheaper than in other fashionable Georgian centres such as Bath or London.

Trains of pack-ponies, each carrying two panniers of coal slung on a wooden saddle, a bushel of coal in each pannier, slowly and laboriously made their way from County Durham to the town, the relatively short distance being reflected in a lower price than elsewhere. This made Richmond ideal for a person such as the Diarist, who appears to be a member of that growing class of the 'middling' sort, not poor but having to be careful with expenditure.

Contemporary improvements in travel are also evident. Frequent journeys between Richmond and Winston in Teesdale were made possible by a brand new bridge across the River Tees. Coaching services using turnpike roads facilitated journeys to York, Cambridge and London. Those making such journeys were prevailed upon to deliver the letters so eagerly awaited, as postal charges had not yet been adjusted to reflect the improved communication systems. Thus fashionable Richmond was in close contact with what was happening in London, and news arriving from the Diarist's family and friends who were based there.

We also see that typically Georgian change whereby the fortunes of many old, established families waned as those of new ones waxed. Of particular importance is remarkably detailed material on the new fashion for educating girls. Readers witness at close quarters the setting up in the town of a school for young ladies, through the eyes of our Diarist, who was seen as an expert at the social skills they required to emerge out into their new world. She tutored the pupils by having them to her rooms to learn the etiquette of Georgian tea drinking and the art of conversation.

A Sense of Place

The Diarist, as many people still do, decided that Richmond was the place to choose to live. We can perhaps infer that, as well as its intrinsic attractive and fashionable qualities, added benefits were its relatively easy journeys to and from her relatives in Winston, and possibly also her family's roots in nearby Easby.

To most people today, despite its quaintness and cherished historic traditions, Richmond seems relatively small and not particularly significant. It is difficult to convey how much that has changed since the eighteenth century, and thus to explain why the Diarist had settled here rather than in some other North Riding town, or elsewhere in the north of England.

Georgian Richmond was not only fashionable, it was relatively large in population, with perhaps 1,800 inhabitants in 1764. The city of York was only about seven times larger. Apart from the coastal port towns of Whitby and Scarborough, and Malton on the navigable River Derwent, Richmond was the largest town in the North Riding. The present county town of Northallerton was then only perhaps three-quarters the size of Richmond, followed by Thirsk at about two-thirds. The nearest market towns of Reeth, Bedale and Leyburn were each about a quarter the size of Richmond, or less.

Richmond was the market town of Swaledale, but in Georgian times that valley was not the pretty postcard rural landscape it is now, rather an often smoky, industrialised centre, dominated by the lead mining industry. Some of the smelted lead passed through the town in packhorse trains heading for the River Tees and sea transport to London, bringing a certain amount of spin-off trade for the town. It also generated hard-fought legal battles, such as the famous Beldi Hill case involving the Diarist's uncle, Thomas Smith of London.

The sheep farming, which is still the mainstay of Swaledale's economy, was then related to another major local industry, the hand-knitting of stockings and caps for export to the Low Countries. The young Caleb Readshaw, who crops up in 'The Richmond Diary', was a member of a family who had made their money as merchants exporting these knitted goods on a large scale, and had built a handsome Georgian townhouse on the proceeds.

If the landscape of Swaledale did not attract the praise of visitors, Richmond itself certainly did. Numerous paintings, sketches and engravings of various sorts, were made to illustrate its beauties in Georgian times. Among the engravings were the *South West Prospect of Richmond in the County of York* and the *North East Prospect of Richmond in the County of York* published by Samuel and Nathaniel Buck in 1749. Below the North East Prospect is printed a lengthy description which includes the text:

> *It* [Richmond] *is a place of good Trade which is daily improving by reason of the late Encouragement given by the Corporation, to Industrious and Ingenious Tradesmen and Mechanicks of all sorts, and from all parts, to settle among them. The Air is extremely Healthful, and the Town generally admired; as well for its Delightful Situation, and great variety of Beautiful and Extensive Prospects.*

The quote sums up many of the concepts which made Richmond so important at the time of 'The Richmond Diary'. It was not a quaint backwater, but a bustling, thriving, prosperous and growing town, attractive to the avant-garde. The corporation was actively encouraging craftsmen with the most modern skills to come and work here to serve, and gain, custom from the new 'middling' class who would be attracted by the healthy air and beautiful situation.

In the 1720s and 1730s the city of York, which had been declining economically, invested heavily in reinventing itself as the leading social centre of the North. The corporation of Richmond, which was arguably already in a relatively stronger position economically than York, soon followed suit, firstly by actively supporting activities of commercial benefit, then by providing social facilities.

In 1744, using something reminiscent of a private finance initiative, they facilitated the building of a large and handsome new toll booth in the market place, replacing an older structure, to serve as the base of the town's trade. Then shortly afterwards, they were instrumental in ensuring that the ecclesiastical courts of the Archdeaconry of Richmond, which brought people to the town from a wide area of the north of England, were housed in improved accommodation in Trinity chapel.

In the mid-1750s the corporation itself financed the building of an elegant assembly room, and they also upgraded the status of the town's horse races, moving these to a new permanent racecourse in 1765. Thus, by the mid-1760s, Richmond was established as a leading provincial social centre, well equipped to offer elegant assemblies and prestigious horse races, as well as hosting spectacular militia musters, and having attractive promenades. No wonder it soon also drew visits by troupes of travelling players and other entertainers – all appear in 'The Richmond Diary'.

Richmond had long been an important trading centre. Not only was there then, as now, the weekly Saturday market, but also three annual fairs (mega trading events) noted by the Diarist. Although she seems not to have been attracted to the town's many antiquarian ruins, she does mention visits to various local scenic attractions, such as the famed landscaped gardens of the Yorke family on The Green, and also the beauty spot near Love Lane Farm below Easby.

As a medieval borough, both the local government and the commerce of Richmond in the 1760s were still run through the town's thirteen ancient craft guilds. The new 'gentlemanly' class moving in to take part in Georgian social life had to belong to one of these guilds if they wished to serve on the corporation and possibly progress to hold the office of mayor. Such men, not having served an apprenticeship to, say, a tanner, nor belonging to a guild through patrimony, had to pay to join a guild in order to gain 'freedom' of the borough, a system called redemption. The Diarist notes some such arrivistes, particularly if they were from the area she clearly knew well.

Not only did the demographic character of the town change in the Georgian period, but also its physical appearance. Many of the town's existing houses were rebuilt, replacing medieval timber-framed buildings with larger and more elegant ones, usually in stone and often of three storeys. Occasionally brick was used in order to make a fashion statement, in Richmond it was a much more expensive material than stone.

The first to be built of brick was the early eighteenth-century town house of Charles Bathurst, which soon became the King's Head Hotel in the market place. Occupying the site of three older houses, it was eight bays long and three storeys high, and must have seemed very out of scale at the time. Behind it was an elaborate pleasure garden called Placendale. The Readshaw family of merchants also built a handsome brick town house, The Grove, with elegant plasterwork and woodwork inside. Its site, near the bottom of Frenchgate, gave its main rooms impressive views down the scenic valley of the river Swale.

Sometimes older houses were simply re-fronted, such as Hill House, or given more fashionable windows, such as that of the Allen family at the bottom of Gallowgate, or the Yorke family's mansion on The Green. A major spur to rebuilding was the capital received if owners sold their ancient parliamentary voting rights to help attain the 'pocket borough' eventually achieved by Sir Lawrence Dundas. The updating of Richmond's town houses, and its public buildings and infrastructure, continued for many years after the mid-1760s, so it is not certain what percentage of the town's houses, even in the fashionable streets of Frenchgate and Newbiggin, had been 'georgianised' at this time.

This poses a problem in deducing where the Diarist and her circle lived. She does not refer to people's houses either as 'newly-built' or 'old-fashioned', even when we know their date – her friend Dr Pringle had built his house on the north side of Newbiggin in 1763, and Mrs Wilson's sister, who lived almost opposite him, had a new house oddly in the Gothick, not the usual classical, style of architecture.

Important Richmond public buildings of medieval date which must have been familiar to the Diarist include the Market Cross in the market place, which would be replaced by the present Market Obelisk in 1771, in conjunction with the provision of an improved public water supply. Another was the bridge crossing the river Swale which, in the mid-1760s, despite carrying the new Richmond-Lancaster turnpike road, was still a narrow structure of four irregular arches. After damage by an enormous flood in 1771, this was superseded by a wider and less steep bridge of three even arches, designed by the bridgemaster of the North Riding, the great York architect John Carr, in 1788–89.

An Example of Period Writing

How important is this particular diary to those who study the Georgian period? The answer is 'very', for it is an example of one which takes us in a different direction from most earlier ones. Diaries were first intended as daily or weekly spiritual records for religious purposes, then became a list of the user's forthcoming activities, or a record of domestic expenditure, and lastly a summary of what had happened during each day. By the mid-eighteenth century the keeping of a diary was commonplace for both men and women. Printers produced huge quantities of such diaries, ready for use. Jane Austen was to call it 'journalising', and 'The Richmond Diary' manuscript is indeed introduced to us as the continuation of a 'Journal'.

Yes, it does summarise the weather, and identify where the Diarist has been and with whom, and even sets down details of illnesses and how they were treated. Yet this journal is of the new sort of Georgian record, in which writers set down how they see the world in which they live, how they interact with people they know, how their personal life is taking shape, even what they want out of it.

In this new concept, mid-eighteenth-century diarists were being encouraged to keep a personal record of their feelings, essentially asserting the validity of self-expression. This is the emergence of 'sensibility', which governed how people behaved, how they reacted to the external world, and essentially how they felt. That, after all, was why so many ventured for the first time into north Yorkshire, and came to see Richmond's landscapes and ruins: to experience what happened when they saw them and reacted to such.

It was also the reason why diarists made a record of whom they visited and who visited them, and for how long, and when, and to whom they wrote their growing numbers of letters and the replies they received. Through these personal encounters, in this emerging and different Georgian world, people learned and grew. Strange though it may seem to us, this is why the hours spent taking tea, their many rendezvous with family and friends, and sometimes strangers, were pivotal, particularly to women. Tea drinking fostered conversation – about anything and everything, serious and otherwise.

'The Richmond Diary' gives a very special period perspective on all this. It is accompanied by another characteristic, the physical form in which it was expressed. The published books of instruction stressed the need for neatness, attention to spelling and punctuation throughout. All of which implied a much greater degree of literacy than had been available previously, and a determination to be exact and precise. In the pages of 'The Richmond Diary' there are hardly any mistakes. As in architecture, design, dress, 'Taste' was highly valued – what something looked like was as important as what it contained – so we clearly have a Georgian writer at work.

Why would this matter if it was just a very personal document, not for circulation even among family and friends? The answer lies in that set of new and emerging terms: not only 'sensibility', but now also 'judgement', 'natural taste' and 'sensitivity'. The Diarist would not wish to produce something so careless that she would be ashamed when she reread it (an increasingly important practise). Much time was spent in its compiling, because a diary was being written for a distant future, for posterity, recording the world in which he or she lived and moved, and where they were heading as an individual.

But there is something else one notices about the way 'The Richmond Diary' is written. It is almost as though individual entries have been revised for a particular effect. The daily encounters are expressed, as the Diarist talks to this person and that person, as though a drama is taking place. We see the same characters making their entrances and exits. And when those bare names are fleshed out – as *Life In Georgian Richmond, North Yorkshire* seeks to demonstrate – it is almost as though this book is not so much a diary as a work of fiction, a novel.

Without the Georgian novel, the historian would know much less about the England, let alone the Yorkshire, of this time. The novel was the literary innovation of the Georgian period, with outstanding novelists from Defoe to Richardson, from Smollet to Sterne. Enthusiasm for their publications swept the country, and their books were read via bookshops and circulating libraries. As a footnote, the Richmond Diarist and her friends were fortunate in having 'Tibby' Tinkler's bookshop in the town.

These novels and their authors were immensely important in this changing Georgian world. Their impact is seen almost everywhere, and quotations from them crop up in the most unlikely places.

For the Richmond Diarist, the most significant novelist – a taste she shared with the later Jane Austen – was Samuel Richardson. His influence is there in the way she organised her daily record, dated entries, labelled her title page, and even perhaps, like her friends, chased after potential marriage partners. One might even suggest that she saw herself as sharing certain characteristics with his most famous leading ladies, *Pamela* (1740) and *Clarissa* (1747). And that is a mid-Georgian compliment she would have enjoyed!

A Woman's Journal

So who was writing this document? We speculate on her likely identity later, and so discuss the Diarist here in more general terms. It is particularly difficult to deduce from the text her likely age. She is old enough to be running her own household, but young enough still to have her 'Mama' living, although they do not seem particularly close. Her father is never mentioned. She has a sister who seems to be younger and is probably often elsewhere. She shows interest in other people's babies and children, but expresses no hope of ever having any of her own.

Nevertheless, implicitly, 'The Richmond Diary' is the record of a search for a husband. The Diarist is learning the ways of the world and applies herself conscientiously to the task of recording her self-education in social skills. She observes how other people behave, in what activities they participate, and how she compares with them.

It seems to the authors that the Diarist has been living in Richmond for some time before the journal starts, but that she had grown up elsewhere. One of the places she refers to as 'home' is the Winston rectory of her Emerson relatives, and if she had grown up there it would explain the very close bond with her Emerson girl cousins. They could all have been educated together, possibly even sharing access to some of the behaviour manuals then in vogue. This would also explain the constant presence in her life of the established Church, for Sunday services and particularly its function as a burial ground for the many people whose departure from earthly life is carefully recorded in the pages of this journal.

'The Richmond Diary' provides a short but intense portrait of a woman fully involved in the most up-to-date Georgian activities. She has a broad range of contacts in the town and knows her way around, but is still learning about life in this increasingly important Georgian social centre. We know she attended the races and assemblies, took scenic walks and visited fashionable shops.

An important feature of the diary is the evidence it provides of how girls were being educated. We hear the gossip learnt over teacups, sometimes even of news brought from London by local men engaged in commerce there.

We also get a real sense of Georgian life for someone with limited financial means. Domestic spending is modest, and costly social activities such as the plays and assemblies are a real treat. Scenic walks, which are free, are particularly enjoyed, and the only regular indulgence is tea drinking for its company and conversation. The household had a single maid, Nanny, who left in February 1765; her sister Betty took over on a trial basis until the May Day, and was seemingly satisfactory because she was kept on.

As one might expect for an apparently single woman, the Diarist's relatives feature large in her life. However, it would seem that the nearest were not necessarily the dearest. Her Mama and sister, though an important part of her life, are not mentioned with particular affection, although she is a dutiful daughter when dealing with her mother's health problems. Neither seem to provide the Diarist with any emotional or financial support. Income is rarely mentioned, but perhaps the somewhat intimidating spectre of uncle Thomas Smith in London played some financial role. The Winston cousins, aunt and uncle, perhaps meant more to her. The four female cousins, especially, bring her degrees of joy and pleasure, even a sense of gaiety, which seem otherwise to have been in short supply. It is close friends upon whom the Diarist depends for emotional support.

The Diarist's Circle

The circle of relatives, friends and acquaintances who flit through the pages of 'The Richmond Diary' are a fascinating mix of characters, old and young, rich and poor, living outside Richmond or in the town, and of the latter, some are well-established and others, incomers. Research into who they might be has revealed some unexpected intermeshing.

In addition to the Diarist's mother, sister, uncles, aunt and cousins, several other names may have been more distantly related. The uncles, aunt and cousins were definitely based outside Richmond. Several of her friends have a connection with Teesdale in general, and a surprising number specifically with the Durham Militia, which was raised in and around Barnard Castle. Although the main, explicit, link is to Winston, the underlying most common implicit connection is actually with Easby.

One man who does not appear in the document in person, but is an important character 'off-stage', is the wealthy Scottish merchant Sir Lawrence Dundas (1712–81), who acquired the Aske Estate and invested heavily in Richmond in order to build up a 'pocket borough'. A highly ambitious man, and hugely successful as a businessman, he is generally best known for his ability to amass a fortune by supplying goods to the British army, and later as a banker. However, he also had an astutely innovative mind, being able to 'think outside the box'. For example, he was a major backer of the Forth & Clyde Canal, which ran through his Kerse estate near Falkirk, and this was highly unusual in accommodating the sea-going vessels of the day, whereas most inland waterways necessitated goods being transferred from ships to canal barges. The civil engineer for this canal was the great John Smeaton of Leeds, one of the many Yorkshiremen who contributed greatly to the Industrial Revolution. Unlike the characters who appear in 'The Richmond Diary', Sir Lawrence Dundas still resonates in present-day Richmond, as his successors still own Aske Hall, having become, first, earls of Zetland, and later, and still, marquesses of Zetland.

Sir Lawrence's influence was a major factor behind many of the changes which occurred in Richmond from the early 1760s onwards. Some of the characters featured in 'The Richmond Diary', including Thomas Cornforth and George Hutchinson, had a clear link to Sir Lawrence, as they came to the town to work on his behalf, particularly on his acquisition of property. Other characters demonstrated smaller-scale business acumen of the type so typical of this part of the Georgian period.

The Diarist has strong friendship ties to some old Richmond families, such as Close, Nicholls and Readshaw, but several other of her friends are people drawn to Richmond by the business opportunities afforded by its growing prosperity. An outsider who became rich from trading in Richmond was the grocer James Newsam who, with his young wife, became close friends with the Diarist. They and the Medcalfs offered her good (and younger) company.

Of the Diarist's older friends, Mrs Mawer was something of a mother figure, encouraging her to improve her position socially and financially, as she herself had done, and to take part in things. Betty Beautyment and Matty Beauly, both hard-working businesswomen, also seem to provide some stability. The Wilsons, who feature prominently, apparently required some support themselves rather than offering it. They provide a particularly fascinating position in the story, representing a new class of business entrepreneurs, as they set about training young women for their emergence into a fresh, alternative world.

'The Richmond Diary' chronicles a major shift occurring within mid-eighteenth-century society. Women, be they spinsters, widows or mothers, could now organise their own activities, in which men played only small parts. Decisions as to whom to meet, where to go, what to do, how to spend their time, are taken by the female participants who make up this Richmond society, and we are shown in great detail how they behave and how they see themselves.

From breakfast, which is rarely mentioned but was probably eaten 7–8 am, until dinner, perhaps about 2 pm, they undertake household tasks – washing, ironing, sewing, gardening. However they have the freedom to drop these when special situations arise – the arrival and entertainment of visiting friends, the races, assemblies, and drama performances.

When dinner, the main meal of the day, had been taken, a very different set of female social functions took over. New rituals now dominated – especially the taking of tea, often around 5pm – and their days were organised around giving and accepting invitations for this Georgian preoccupation. The Diarist sets out in detail how this led to other, new, participatory activities – going for walks, going to see friends, talking together in pairs or in friendly groups. This post-dinner period is recorded in a surprising amount of detail. It was clearly a significant time which must not be wasted. It could last until bedtime, which in the Diarist's case seems to have been about 10 pm.

The entries illustrate how women spent time among themselves – going to the shops, meeting new people, and entertaining visitors from elsewhere. A new language takes over: they 'call upon'; they 'come in'; they 'went in': all terms relating to an emerging set of conventions.

'The Richmond Diary' also shows that the Diarist and her contemporaries engaged in different Richmond activities from those of the older generation. Mama was, for much of the time, invisible – either elsewhere, or perhaps tucked away in an upstairs room. When she appears, it is to participate in her old-fashioned sequences, strictly with women of her own age, or pursuing with her daughter practices which they would know were out-dated.

People: The Diarist's Family

Mama

The widowed mother of the Diarist (and her sister) flits enigmatically in and out of the pages of 'The Richmond Diary'. For more than half of the time she seems not to be present in the household. She is rarely associated with the Diarist and her circle for tea and conversation, she never invites anyone to join her to take tea, she is not available to meet visiting Emerson nieces, nor even for the visit of their mother, her sister-in-law. The only social gatherings in which she participates are those with Mrs Mawer and, to a lesser extent, Mrs Wilson.

She does not join in with the popular activity of visiting the shops, perhaps due to infirmity, or poverty, and, like the widowed Mrs Mawer, she removes herself from attendance at the races. Indeed she cannot be in residence during the races because there would be no room for her when so many visitors were present. Her name is given to a room in the Diarist's house, possibly on an upstairs floor, but only when it is being used as sick quarters, probably due to its fireplace being easier or cheaper to use than those in other rooms.

She plays no part in the running of the house, and even when the Diarist returns after her two-month stay at Winston, Mama is not mentioned as one of those who welcomes her back. Her dealings with the Diarist are restricted to very short walks, and a rare attendance at a Sunday church service or Friday morning prayers. She receives four – apparently significant – letters (from the London Smiths) but she does not reply to any of them. Instead she orders the Diarist to send the mysterious certificates to her uncle Smith in London. Uncle Smith would eventually bequeath Mama £100 in his will, a smaller amount than most of the legacies to his relatives, even though she was a widow. So he would seem not to value her highly.

All of which leads to the conclusion that, not only did she have no role in the Richmond circle that her elder daughter was building up, but also that she was treated almost as a pariah, condemned to live a more isolated life than many other widows in Richmond. What had she done wrong?

Sister

The Diarist's sister does not make many appearances in 'The Richmond Diary'. However she plays an important role in the narrative and is another example of the changing world of women which the document records. She seems to be younger than the Diarist, and usually only makes an appearance on Saturdays and Sundays, apparently not living in the same Richmond house, although there is no clue as to a different residence. Perhaps her weekly activities make full use of her time.

She is certainly registered as a family member, and invitations to the family invariably include her, although she never takes them up and is never involved in running family errands. Perhaps her role is providing a background to family activity, and she may sometimes be among the 'us' who took tea.

However, she is closely involved in family communications, receiving letters from, and sending letters to, the same relatives and friends as does her sister and, to a much smaller degree, their mother. Correspondence arrives for her at the Diarist's Richmond address, and she replies when she is available, not necessarily promptly.

Significantly, she never takes part in Richmond's social activities such as the races, assemblies and dances, or even church attendance, and she is never recorded meeting family members or visitors. Her letters do not involve making arrangements for such visits.

The Smith Family

One of the few biographical certainties of the Diarist's life is that she was a member of the Smith family. She explicitly mentions several relatives called Smith, including uncle Thomas Smith, Nanny Smith and also Minny Smith. The family probably originated in Richmond but by the early eighteenth century had closer links with Easby. They were a scholarly lot, and produced several clerics, but often seem to have experienced extremes of wealth and penury. Several family members returned to Easby in their old age, thus probably joining in activities in Richmond circles, before being buried at Easby.

A seventeenth-century Dr William Smith married Anne Layton of West Layton, a small village just north of the A66 west of Stanwick. The family subsequently not only used the names

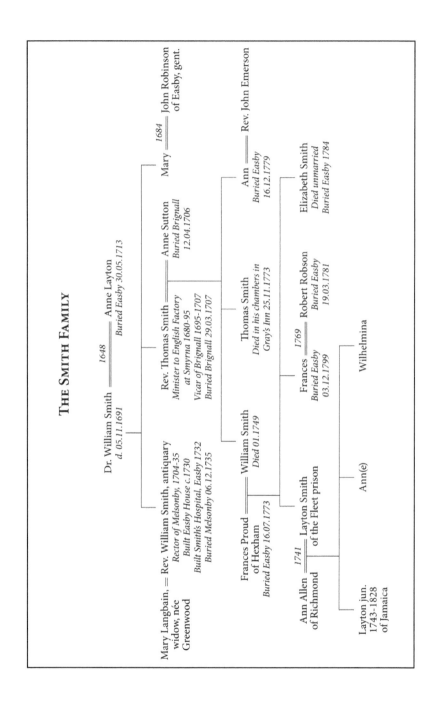

THE SMITH FAMILY

Dr. William Smith ═══1648═══ Anne Layton
d. 05.11.1691   Buried Easby 30.05.1713

Rev. Thomas Smith ═══ Anne Sutton   Mary ═══1684═══ John Robinson
Minister to English Factory   Buried Brignall   of Easby, gent.
at Smyrna 1680-95   12.04.1706
Vicar of Brignall 1695-1707
Buried Brignall 29.03.1707

Mary Langbain, ═ Rev. William Smith, antiquary   Thomas Smith   Ann ═══ Rev. John Emerson
widow, née   Rector of Melsonby, 1704-35   Died in his chambers in   Buried Easby
Greenwood   Built Easby House c.1730   Gray's Inn 25.11.1773   16.12.1779
Built Smith's Hospital, Easby 1732
Buried Melsonby 06.12.1735

Frances Proud ═══ William Smith   Frances ═══1769═══ Robert Robson   Elizabeth Smith
of Hexham   Died 01.1749   Buried Easby   Buried Easby   Died unmarried
Buried Easby 16.07.1773   03.12.1799   19.03.1781   Buried Easby 1784

Ann Allen ═══1741═══ Layton Smith   Ann(e)   Wilhelmina
of Richmond   of the Fleet prison

Layton jun.
1743-1828
of Jamaica

William and Thomas over and over again, but also Ann(e) and
Layton. Dr William and Anne Smith had four children, William,
Thomas, Mary (who married a John Robinson) and Ann. This
second William was a Senior Fellow at University College, Oxford
and then became Rector of Melsonby, near Scotch Corner, which
had links with the College. At Melsonby he built a handsome
Queen Anne rectory, and there in his study assembled material on
the history of University College and other antiquarian subjects.

In 1729 Revd William Smith purchased the manor of Easby and
built for himself a fashionable early Georgian residence, originally
called Easby House but now often referred to as Easby Hall, and
also endowed an almshouse, the Smith Hospital, in 1732. He died
in 1735 at the age of 85 and was buried at Melsonby. As he had no
children he left his antiquarian papers and the Easby property to
his nephew, a third William, son of his brother Thomas.

Thomas was also a clergyman and was employed by the Levant
Company to serve as minister to the large English population at the
'factory' or trading post at Smyrna (now Ismir) in Turkey, before
returning to England as vicar of Brignall on the south side of
Teesdale from 1695 until his death in 1707. Revd Thomas Smith's
three children, William, Thomas and Ann, were probably born
while he was in Smyrna. This third William was almost certainly
the Diarist's father, and Thomas, the Diarist's formidable uncle
in London. Ann became the wife of Revd John Emerson, rector of
Winston.

This last William was a bright boy who became a scholar at
St Peter's School, Westminster, a very young student at Oxford,
and was admitted to Gray's Inn in 1720. He was, however, soon
in financial difficulties and, to raise funds, sold the antiquarian
papers of his uncle, Revd William Smith, some of which were later
presented to the Society of Antiquaries. He obtained little for them,
and his debts weighed heavily on him. His health deteriorated and
he retired to Easby where he died in his mid-fifties in January
1749. He married a Hexham lady, Frances Proud, and they had
three children, Layton, Frances (the most likely candidate for
the Diarist) and Elizabeth (the Diarist's sister). Frances Proud,
presumably 'Mama', outlived him by many years, being buried at
Easby as 'Frances widow of William Smith Esqr late of Easby' on
16 July 1773.

Uncle Thomas Smith was a key player in a major long-running
saga in the history of Swaledale. After his education at Richmond
Grammar School he was admitted to Gray's Inn on 23 June 1718,
and continued to live in London for the rest of his life. However, in

1738 he purchased the Swaledale manors of Healaugh and Muker, which had been put on the market by trustees trying to settle the late and last Duke of Wharton's debts. Intense interest from several potential purchasers raised the price, and Smith ended up paying £10,500, much more than he had intended, and he had to ask for time to raise £7,000 of the money. Confusion over exactly what the trustees ultimately conveyed to Smith led to the Beldi Hill Dispute, one of the most extraordinary court cases of the eighteenth century.

It began with a boundary dispute between Thomas Smith and Lord Pomfret, the owner of adjacent land, over who had the mineral rights to a rich vein of lead lying underground at Beldi Hill near Keld in a remote part of Swaledale. During prolonged acrimony between the two parties, miners employed by both sides were instructed to commence workings on the disputed lead, resulting in riotous disorder, criminal damage to equipment and physical assault on a most surprising scale.

Legal action eventually began in 1769 and continued for several years. Large numbers of Swaledale residents provided sworn statements, and many were provided with transport to give evidence to the ensuing court hearings. The first was held in the Quarter Sessions court of the North Riding, followed by a jury trial at the York assizes of 1770, which found in favour of Smith.

In 1771 Pomfret successfully appealed to the House of Lords, and late in 1772 a second jury trial was held at the bar of the court of King's Bench in Westminster Hall, before two of the most senior judges in the land. The Attorney General, and the Solicitor General, both in their private capacities, represented the two sides, quite an event for a matter which concerned a remote part of Swaledale. The verdict again found for Smith, although by this time he was nearing the end of his long life. The prolonged case achieved notoriety in the newspapers, and when Smith died at his chambers in Gray's Inn aged 80, in 1773, there was much speculation as to his wealth, how much the court cases had cost him, and how much the victory had gained him. Pomfret, his opponent, was a broken man financially.

Thomas Smith's will, which he had made in 1769, shows that he was then already worth many thousands of pounds. He made his brother-in-law Revd John Emerson his executor and gave him a legacy of £500. A codicil of 1771 gave Emerson an additional bequest of £100 for the help he had given at the York trial. Thomas's sister Ann Emerson was left £500, as were each of her daughters, his nieces. Two other nieces, daughters of his brother William, also received £500 each, two great-nieces £500 between them, and his great-nephew Layton Smith junior was left £1,000. These legacies are likely to have been life changing, but 'The Richmond Diary' stops several years earlier.

In 1746, many years before 'The Richmond Diary' starts, Thomas Smith had bought the family's Easby property from his indebted older brother William, and William's son Layton Smith senior, to help them financially. This was after taking legal action against them in Chancery in 1743 over money they owed him, some of which debts went back many years earlier. Thomas Smith had no legitimate descendants. Rather than leaving the Easby estate to any of his Smith relatives, his will left it to his illegitimate son Thomas King, who changed his name to Smith, and he also made generous provision for two illegitimate daughters and grandchildren.

Even before his celebrated victory in the Beldi Hill Dispute, Thomas Smith was highly regarded in his professional life as a lawyer. In 'The Richmond Diary' he comes over as a figure held in some awe, perhaps even fear, to whom the Diarist was instructed by her Mama on three occasions to send some mysterious 'certificates'. We have been unable to decide what these were, but one possibility is that they were connected with the build-up to the Beldi Hill court cases.

Layton Smith the elder obtained notoriety of a different sort. In December 1736, following in the footsteps of his father and uncle, he was admitted to Gray's Inn, as the son and heir of William Smith of Easby, county of York, esquire. He was probably only about 16 years old, so it would seem he went there to finish off his education with some exposure to the law, rather than with the intention of training for a career at the bar. Five years later, presumably on his majority, while still in London, he married Ann Allen, sister of William Allen of Richmond, probably the 'Nanny Smith' of 'The Richmond Diary'.

Layton seems to have speculated in various business ventures, and would later be described as a merchant, dealer and chapman (or trader). In 1749 he obtained a Crown grant of the office of water bailiff of the Thames 'from the great bridge at Staines to the head of that river, including all the branches and rivulets that fall into it, to be held during His Majesty's pleasure'. This sinecure was revoked by the Crown in August 1760, probably because Layton Smith had by then become bankrupt and a prisoner in the Fleet Prison.

It is not clear how much his bankruptcy was due to his father's poor financial circumstances, or his own rash investments.

Certainly his uncle Thomas was scathing about him in his will, leaving him an annuity of just £50 with the damning explanation:

> [M]*y Nephew Layton Smith the Elder has by folly and Extravagance* [got] *through a very handsome Fortune of his own and has obstinately chosen to Submit to a Shamefull Bankruptcy and although his behaviour towards me has been very Bad and my advice at all times totally disregarded so that he is far from meriting any favour from me yet out of regard to our Relationship being unwilling wholly to desert him.*

Layton Smith became a well-known prisoner in the Fleet. When taken there under protest he made a solemn vow never to shave his beard until his release. As he was there for many years, his beard grew so long that John Faber engraved his portrait. One of the published versions has a caption describing how Layton had looked after some of his fellow prisoners who were suffering during an outbreak of a contagious fever, so it would seem he had some public sympathy.

Both Layton Smith's sisters were included in the will of their uncle Thomas Smith. Like Frances, dealt with later in 'Who is the Diarist?', the other sister's bequest was given as 'to my niece Elizabeth Smith the sum of five hundred pounds'. Elizabeth died unmarried, and was buried at Easby in 1784. The two sisters are likely to have suffered under the shadow of their brother's imprisonment in the Fleet. His debts and shame probably formed much of the content of the various letters sent by, and to, his wife Nanny Smith. The Diarist notes the receipt of 15s for some of Layton's books.

Layton senior and his wife Ann/Nanny had three children, Layton, Ann and Wilhelmina. Layton junior (1743–1828) made his career in Jamaica, possibly travelling there on the strength of his £1,000 legacy. He was among the subscribers to a petition concerning relief after the island suffered a dreadful storm in January 1781, and at some stage had an illegitimate child with a local woman there.

Ann and Wilhelmina were presumably the granddaughters, to each of whom Mama sent a half-crown by their uncle Mr Allen, and doubtless were grateful for the £500 they shared under the will of their great-uncle Thomas Smith. Wilhelmina – Minny and Mina in 'The Richmond Diary' – must have spent at least some time in Richmond as she was involved in the sale of some of the property of her uncle William Allen to Sir Lawrence Dundas in 1767.

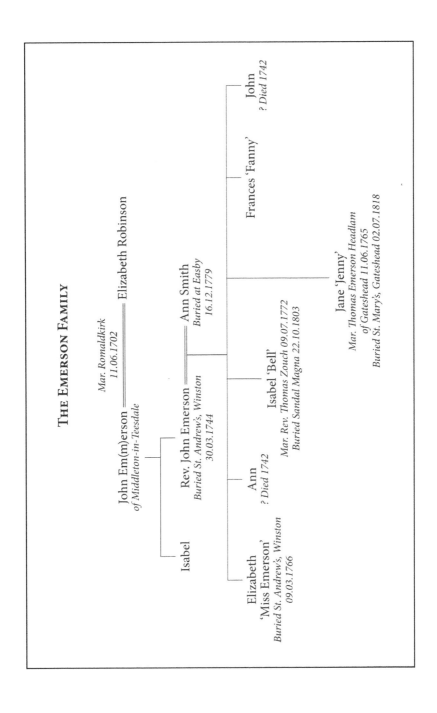

The Emerson Family

The Emersons of Winston in Teesdale played a large part in the Diarist's life. They were related through Ann (née Smith), her paternal aunt, who had married Revd John Emerson (1705–74), at the time of 'The Richmond Diary' the rector of Winston. John and Ann's daughters are referred to as the Diarist's cousins. The Emerson household is one of the places the Diarist refers to as 'home', so she, and her sister, might have grown up with their Emerson relations.

The name Emerson was common in County Durham in general and Teesdale in particular, and this John Emerson came from Middleton-in-Teesdale. His parents, John Emerson of Middleton-in-Teesdale and Elizabeth Robinson, married at Romaldkirk on 11 June 1702, and the family was living at Middleton-in-Teesdale when his elder sister Isabel was baptised in 1703, and himself likewise on 19 May 1705. After Lincoln College, Oxford, he was ordained and held several livings, some in plurality – curate of Edmondbyers (County Durham) 1728–39, rector of Middleton-in-Teesdale 1730–74, rector of Stainton (in the Cleveland area of north Yorkshire) 1749–54 and eventually rector of Winston 1754–74.

Revd John Emerson and his wife had six children while living at Middleton-in-Teesdale. After his appointment to Winston, the family moved to the rectory there. Four Emerson daughters – Elizabeth, Isabel, Jane and Frances – feature prominently in 'The Richmond Diary'. Letters were exchanged between the Diarist and her sister and the various Emerson cousins, and they often came to stay with the Diarist, particularly for the week of the annual Richmond race meeting.

The eldest child, Elizabeth, born in 1732, is always referred to by the Diarist as Miss Emerson, without a Christian name, according to eighteenth-century etiquette. She had returned from London in June 1765 and attended the Richmond races held that September. Although there is no reference in the 'The Richmond Diary' to her being in poor health, she sadly died on 27 February 1766, soon after it ends. She was buried at Winston on 9 March, the ten-day gap presumably due to her body having to be brought some distance, perhaps from London. Her name and date of death were included on the later brass plaque in the chancel floor of Winston church commemorating her father.

Isabel, born in 1735 and known to the Diarist as 'Bell', would, in 1772, marry Revd Dr Thomas Zouch (1737–1815), prebendary of Durham and rector of Wycliffe-on-Tees. A botanist, antiquary and writer, he wrote a life of Isaak Walton. Childless, they retired to his native Sandal Magna near Wakefield, where Isabel was buried on 22 October 1803. He remarried, and when he died his old friend and fellow scholar James Tate, the Richmond schoolmaster, composed the Latin text for his memorial in Sandal Church.

Jane, born in 1737 and known as 'Jenny', married Thomas Emerson Headlam of Gateshead. From his middle name he was presumably a distant relative. Thomas and Jane had a large family, one of whom, John, went, like his grandfather, to Lincoln College, Oxford. After also taking Holy Orders, he succeeded his uncle as rector of Wycliffe from 1793, and later became archdeacon of Richmond.

Jenny's wedding on 11 June 1765 is mentioned in 'The Richmond Diary', though the Diarist did not attend, despite having bought a new hat just three days beforehand! A few days later she received a piece of wedding cake through Jenny's sister Frances, known as 'Fanny', and younger by two years. Fanny seems to have been a particularly lively cousin, not only eagerly attending the races and the associated assemblies, but achieving the accolade of riding up to the racecourse in Mr Witham's coach.

Revd John Emerson lived on until 1774 despite being very ill in March 1765. He was a man highly thought of by his fearsome brother-in-law, the London lawyer Thomas Smith, who bequeathed him £500, plus £100 in a codicil to his will. Ann Emerson would have to vacate Winston rectory after her husband's death, and seems to have returned to her roots in Easby, for she was buried there on 16 December 1779 as 'Mrs Anne Emmerson of Easby, widow of the late Rev'd John Emmerson, Rector of Winston'. Doubtless it was not only her family links, but also the genteel social events on offer in Richmond, plus the company of many respectable widows, especially those of clergymen, that encouraged her to settle there.

The various Mr Allens

Three Mr Allens, seemingly all of the same family, occur in 'The Richmond Diary' – 'Mr Allen', 'Mr F. Allen' and 'Old Mr Allen'. Mr Allen was based in London but called on the Diarist soon after returning to Richmond and again just before leaving. He made frequent visits to her home when in residence, though he never seems to drink tea. Mr F. Allen was based in Richmond and occasionally came for tea. Letters from and to the Diarist's family travelled by Mr Allen, and letters to Mr F. Allen were sometimes enclosed with letters received by the Diarist. Old Mr Allen drank tea once, and died towards the end of 'The Richmond Diary'.

Related to the Diarist by marriage, the Allens were an important and prosperous Richmond family over several generations. William Allen, a Richmond mercer in the second quarter of the seventeenth century, was followed by his son Francis, whose long life ensured that he was active for the whole of the second half of that century. His business success meant that he was able to endow a charity to help young people set up in business in the town, and to make generous bequests to his widow, five surviving children and several grandchildren.

William, the eldest son of Francis, became a clergyman in Norfolk in the early eighteenth century and, unmarried, endowed two scholarships from Richmond Grammar School to Trinity Hall College, Cambridge. The second son, George, remained in Richmond as another mercer, holding office as mayor in 1703 and 1714, and acquired Oglethorpe House, the large residence at the junction of Pottergate and Gallowgate.

The third son, another Francis, probably the Old Mr Allen in 'The Richmond Diary', also had a very long and active life, remaining childless but providing generously for many of his relatives. The youngest son was John, who seems to have followed a different occupation and also to have been the only member of his generation of the family to have children. He inherited property, including Oglethorpe House, from his brothers William and George.

John's eldest son, yet another Francis, is probably the Mr F. Allen in 'The Richmond Diary'. Based in Manchester when his uncle Revd William Allen of Norfolk made his will in 1730, he was a member of Gray's Inn when he and his wife Bridget sold Oglethorpe House to his younger brother William in 1760. However, he seems to have had a Richmond base as he received some strawberries from the Diarist in July 1765, and she delivered to him letters sent from London.

John's second son, another William, joined the Fellmongers' Guild in 1753 and became an officer in the North York Militia, in which capacity he was involved in quelling a riot in 1757. He spent most of his adult life in London however, being appointed as a 'gentleman usher and daily waiter', at a salary of £150, to the household of the young Queen Charlotte in 1761. He is probably the Mr Allen of 'The Richmond Diary', arriving from London in 1765 on 3 May, and staying till 29 May, coming back on 25 July and remaining in Richmond until 21 October that year.

John Allen also had daughters. Ursula, single and London-based, and at whose home her brother William died in 1786, was the executrix for her uncle Francis. Ann became the Diarist's sister-in-law when she married the elder Layton Smith, and as Nanny Smith in 'The Richmond Diary', had a difficult life in London as the wife of a debtor in the Fleet Prison.

People: The Diarist's Friends

Mrs Mawer & Miss Mawer

Mrs Mawer and her daughter feature prominently in this story. The Diarist sees a great deal of them and holds them in particularly high regard. 'The Richmond Diary' includes them with more familiarity than other regular entries – Mrs Mawer is sometimes simply 'Mrs M.', and the daughter just 'Miss', her Christian name is not given. They were better off financially than the Diarist.

Hannah Mawer was the widow of Revd Dr John Mawer, vicar of Middleton Tyas, a scholar of biblical languages in particular, who had died the year before the diary begins. Having had to vacate the Middleton Tyas vicarage, which he had built, she became one of the many well-to-do widows who moved into rented accommodation in fashionable Georgian Richmond.

John Mawer (1703–63) came from Upleatham in Cleveland, where he inherited property, and was educated at the nearby Kirkleatham Grammar School. After graduating from Trinity College, Cambridge, he was ordained priest in 1727 and two years later, in York Minster, married Hannah Cotesworth, the widow of a wealthy coal owner, who had a young daughter, Henrietta.

John Mawer was appointed vicar of Middleton Tyas in 1731, and also Perpetual Curate of Crathorne in Cleveland in 1732. Middleton Tyas did not have a parsonage at that time, so John and Hannah lived at Crathorne and their children were born there, first John, then Bridget and Kay. Both sons attended Scorton Grammar School, not far from Middleton Tyas, and both followed their father to Trinity and into the Church of England.

John Mawer senior had progressed his career in many directions, graduating as a doctor of divinity from Edinburgh University in January 1736, and from 1750 exploiting the deposits of copper ore discovered on the glebe lands at Middleton Tyas. He is commemorated in the chancel of Middleton Tyas church by a wall monument, which has a gushing inscription noting his scholarship and linguistic feats.

Hannah, who had presumably inherited money from her first husband, was left £100 in his will charged on his Upleatham estate, also his plate, linen and household goods for life. Sons John and Kay were left his books, which were to be equally divided between them, and Kay also received a bequest of £500. Bridget was appointed executrix and received all his other real and personal estate.

In the mid–1760s Hannah was an elderly lady of about 70, so presumably more contemporary with the Diarist's mother than herself. Whatever the relationship, she was clearly someone on whom the Diarist greatly depended socially, and her being unwell at the beginning of August 1764 caused great concern.

Bridget Mawer was a financially independent unmarried woman in her mid-thirties, but there is no hint of a sisterly or close relationship with the Diarist, although they visited the shops together. Bridget moved in higher social circles, mixing with the Yorke family in Richmond, and in January 1765 she spent a week at Raby castle near Staindrop in County Durham, then the seat of Henry Vane, second Lord Darlington, and his wife Margaret Lowther. No reason for the visit is given, and she went not with the Diarist, but another friend, Mrs Panton. Kay Mawer makes four appearances in 'The Richmond Diary', first sending Mama a moorcock, which he had presumably shot, and then being present at tea with his mother and/or sister on three occasions.

The two Mawer ladies provide interesting news for the Diarist, having their portraits 'taken' by an artist referred to as 'Pickerin'. This phonetic version of the name the Diarist has heard almost certainly relates to Henry Pickering, a well-known portrait painter working in northern circles – and one of some quality, having been on a Grand Tour. There are several of his paintings in the York area.

Bridget Mawer was painted late in July 1764 and Hannah a few weeks later in September, when the artist had taken a shop in Richmond for the temporary display of his work, which the Diarist visited, doubtless being suitably impressed. Not only would acquiring such portraits confirm the Mawers' superior financial status over her own but, even if less than full-length likenesses, a sizeable and gracious home in which to hang them is also implicit. This is a period when more women were having their portraits painted, as their economic and social status increased relative to that of men, and this doubtless brought artists such as Henry Pickering more work.

Part way through 'The Richmond Diary', Hannah and Bridget Mawer moved to Gainford, a large and imposing village on the north side of the river Tees, not far from Winston. Gainford has an attractive village green and several splendid properties, a large and historic church, next to which is a vast former parsonage, and it had a spa. Trinity College, Cambridge, was the patron of the living, so the Mawers may have had a connection with the church there.

It would seem that the move was initiated by Bridget Mawer, who paid two preliminary visits before the pair finally moved in May 1765. The Diarist visited them in their new home when she was at Winston at the end of June. Bridget returned to Richmond on a few occasions, on one of these we are told she was staying on The Green, the mansion of the Yorke family.

One senses that the Diarist must have missed the two Mawers greatly; they had played such an important part of her life in Richmond. Hannah Mawer died in Gainford at the end of 1766, after the diary ends, and was buried with her second husband in Middleton Tyas church.

Mr & Mrs Wilson

The Wilsons, together and separately, feature prominently in 'The Richmond Diary' and are very close to the Diarist. Indeed they, with the Mawers, welcome her back when she returns in January 1765 after spending two months with the Emerson family in Winston.

In the first few pages Mrs Wilson makes the occasional social appearance, but in mid-September 1764 Mr Wilson appears with a Mr Rumney, making enquiries about getting a house for himself, having temporarily got two or three rooms at William Morgotroy's. Mr Wilson is sufficiently close to stay overnight in the Diarist's household, and within a few days it becomes apparent that Mr Wilson is setting up a girls' boarding school in Richmond and is looking not only for premises, but also to recruit teaching staff and pupils.

By the end of January 1765 he could entertain the Diarist to tea at his premises, but no hint is given as to whether this was still at William Morgotroy's, or whether he had found better premises. Certainly the Wilsons' base is near enough to the Diarist's home for frequent visits by each to the other.

The Wilsons are always referred to as Mr Wilson and Mrs Wilson, the Diarist giving us no hint as to their Christian names. Fortunately 'The Richmond Diary' provides one significant clue about Mrs Wilson. We are told that on 9 July 1765 her two sisters, Mrs Raw and Mrs Croft, and her aunt Mrs Barker, drank tea with 'us'. This has led to the discovery that the three sisters were the daughters of Thomas Johnson of Barnard Castle, one of many links between the Diarist and the Teesdale area.

The eldest sister, Hannah, born in 1730, married James Croft and lived in York. The second, Mary, two years younger, married Leonard Raw in Richmond in 1753, and they built and lived in what is now 47 Newbiggin. The Diarist does not mention visits to the Raws' house, although Hannah could have been staying here when the sisters came for tea.

It was the youngest Johnson sister, Ann, born in 1734, who became Mrs Wilson. Her husband, Thomas, had links with the Smith family of Easby, and is mentioned in 1748 as a schoolmaster there. In that year he was married at Easby, his first wife being Anne Raw of Grinton, so he was already connected with that family before his future sister-in-law married into it. Ann Johnson was a younger second wife. It would seem that he had no children by either lady.

When Leonard Raw made his will in 1784, Thomas Wilson had already died. 'Mr Thomas Wilson of Richmond' was buried at Easby on 10 October 1777. His table tomb in Easby churchyard states that he died on 7 October 1777 in the fifty-seventh year of his age. This would make him in his mid-forties in April 1765 when the Diarist notes that he was very lame with rheumatism. The Wilsons make the story of 'The Richmond Diary' particularly interesting, due to the details provided of the process of setting up their school. That it was a school for 'young ladies' is highly apposite for this period of growth in female education, and the Wilsons were obviously entrepreneurs, seeing a business opportunity and successfully exploiting it. That the Diarist played such a key role in the venture also tells us much about her skills.

The Newsams

Mr and Mrs Newsam can be positively identified. 'The Richmond Diary' mentions their new baby boy in early July 1765, and the Richmond parish registers record the baptism on 1 July of William, son of Mr James Newsam. A tombstone in the churchyard provides further information which corroborates other sources. He was buried in 1800 aged 73, and his wife Betty in 1818 aged 81, suggesting that James was 37 in 1764, and Betty about ten years younger.

James Newsam (sometimes spelled Newsham) was a grocer on the High Row, in premises the third along from the corner of Finkle Street, and thus next door to Faith Dixon's establishment. He came from a well-established family of mercers in Yarm, then an important river port on the Tees. Being from outside Richmond, but seeking to trade in the growing and prosperous Georgian town, he had purchased his 'freedom' in the Guild of Mercers, Grocers and Haberdashers in January 1757, and swiftly progressed to serve as warden of the company in 1762. Membership of the guild also allowed him to serve on the corporation, though he remained a member of the Common Council and did not move up to alderman.

James Newsam was probably still single when 'The Richmond Diary' starts. The first reference to him comes very soon after it begins, when the Diarist went into the market place with Bridget Mawer to see 'at Mr Newsham's' the 'tumbler' performing one market day late in July 1764. There are subsequent references to the Diarist and her Emerson cousins spending time in the company of a Mrs Newsam before James apparently married, so perhaps he had brought his mother with him to Richmond. His wife is noted as 'The Bride Mrs Newsham' on 12 September. The couple did not marry in Richmond, and their marriage elsewhere has not yet been traced. The only hint about Betty Newsam's background comes in February 1765 when she had to break off from a tea party having been sent for from her home because her father had been taken ill.

On Sundays, and holy days such as Good Friday 1765, and some summer evenings, the Diarist joined the Medcalfs and the Newsams on walks, for example to Easby. This seems to have taken place both shortly before, and not long after, the birth of William. But it was with Mrs Newsam that the Diarist spent most time, not only drinking tea but also attending the play (seemingly a mainly female pastime) and going to the 'Rood' or 'Beast Fair' in September 1765. The links with the Newsams run right through the whole diary, but there is no record of purchasing any grocery items – not even tea – from that shop!

The Medcalfs

Mr and Mrs Medcalf seem to have been a youngish couple, apparently contemporary with the Newsams. The Medcalfs and the Newsams go for scenic walks on Sundays, to Aske, Easby and the Yorke Gardens. Mrs Medcalf, Mrs Newsam and the Diarist attended the play together and also the Dancing School show.

It is likely that this Mr Medcalf is Bernard Metcalfe, the deputy registrar of the Archdeaconry of Richmond's Consistory Court from 1761 to 1788. He came from the well-known Wensleydale family of Metcalfe, and in 1763 had married Jane, daughter of Tristram Hogg, a family which would later have a Richmond branch. A witness to the marriage in Aysgarth church was James Newsam of Richmond, grocer. James's brother Robert, a Yarm mercer, had married Bernard's sister Elizabeth, so the two couples were related by marriage. Bernard and Jane Metcalfe had several children between 1764 and 1777, starting with George baptised 20 September 1764, in the period covered by 'The Richmond Diary', but before the couple are mentioned in it.

'Mrs Medcalf widow' who drank tea with the Diarist and Mr F. Allen on 12 April 1765 may be Eleanor, the widow of Dr John Metcalfe. John was the son of a wealthy Richmond apothecary, Thomas Metcalfe, and became a prosperous doctor in London. After he became ill there he returned to Richmond where he died in 1760 aged only 46. There is a monument with fulsome Latin inscription to him in St Mary's church. John's brother Thomas, like their father, also moved to London. Such was the surprising amount of travel between Richmond and the capital in the eighteenth century.

The Readheads

In the early part of 'The Richmond Diary', Mrs Readhead is mentioned frequently. She is often at Mrs Mawer's, and sometimes comes in and sits with the Diarist, only occasionally do the Diarist and her Mama go and take tea with her. It would seem that Mrs Readhead was the Diarist's landlady, for on Friday 19 July 1765 the Diarist paid her the half-year's rent of £5 which had been due on May Day. Perhaps the late payment caused a rift, for there is only one further mention of the name. This time is the only implication that there was a Mr Readhead – 'Readheads has got a family to board, their names Townsend', on Wednesday, 9 October 1765.

There were in the mid-eighteenth century three Readhead brothers in Richmond – Thomas, James and John, and all are known to have lived in Frenchgate, where the Diarist seems to have been based. Thomas and John had been innholders in the 1750s (John at the King's Head Hotel). Thomas and his wife Isabella (Brown) had children baptised between 1740 and 1755, and John was on the Common Council of Richmond corporation.

'James Redhead' had married Elizabeth Glenton in Richmond on 9 June 1734, and he was one of the occupiers of Bowes Hall, a large rambling building set back from the west side of Frenchgate, which would be pulled down about 1785. The implication that Elizabeth Readhead was the Diarist's landlady has led to the inference that the Diarist's accommodation was in part of Bowes Hall. The building was large enough for the Mawers to have another part of it, into which the Townsends moved after Mrs Mawer and her daughter moved to Gainford that May.

On 27 June 1765 the Diarist attended the funeral of James and Elizabeth Readhead's son-in-law, coincidentally called Robert Bowes. 'Robert Bows [*sic*], a soldier in his Grace the Duke of Richmond's Regiment', had married 'Sarah Redhead spinster' on 12 February 1761 by licence. Robert and Sarah/Sally Bowes had two children, Elizabeth baptised 21 January 1762, and Sarah baptised 8 April 1764. Sally visited the Diarist with these very young children on 17 September 1764. 'Mrs Bowes' is also mentioned in 'The Richmond Diary' in connection with the display to the town of the famous Gold Cup trophy won at Richmond races earlier that September.

The Nicholls Family

The family of Nichol/Nicholl/Nicholls/Nickhols was well established in Richmond, unlike many of the Diarist's circle who seem, like her, to have been relative newcomers. For several generations the Nicholls were fellmongers, and as leading tradesmen in the town, served on the corporation and held office as mayor.

Five members of the family occur in 'The Richmond Diary'. Mr Nicholls, mentioned only once, was Henry Nicholls, who served on the corporation as a member of the Common Council but did not proceed to alderman or mayor. Born in 1711, to a father of the same name, he married about 1737 and his marriage settlement survives. At the time of 'The Richmond Diary' he was in a precarious financial position, having mortgaged some of his property and later had a judgement given against him, which was probably why he did not continue to hold public office in the town.

His wife, always respectfully referred to in 'The Richmond Diary' as Mrs Nicholls, had been Ann Wilson, probably from Catterick, and she may have been related to Thomas Wilson. Henry and Ann Nicholls had ten children baptised in Richmond Parish Church between 1738 and 1752, though several died in infancy.

The eldest child was Christopher, born 1738. He attended Richmond Grammar School, and was one of the first pupils under the distinguished headmastership of Anthony Temple to get a university place. He was later ordained and held various appointments in the Ely diocese. His first appointment was a curacy in Cambridge, and this is where he was at the time of 'The Richmond Diary'. Deferentially termed 'the Revd Mr Nichols', he was back in Richmond for the first few months of 1765, and visited the Diarist four times before returning to Cambridge.

The next child, daughter Alice, born 1739 was thus aged 25 when 'The Richmond Diary' starts. She was clearly a close friend of the Diarist, although she lived in London, and from there corresponded with the Diarist and her sister. Alice arrived from London late in June 1765 and spent the rest of that year in Richmond before returning to the capital at the end of December. During those six months she visited the Diarist fifteen times, always spending a considerable time, usually a whole evening.

Elizabeth, the fifth baby born into the family in 1743, features to a lesser extent. Known as Betty, she too lived far enough away to communicate by letter, though there is no indication as to where. She only wrote to the Diarist's sister. Betty was sometimes in Richmond too, and visited the Diarist a few times.

The Beautyments

The Beautyment family lived at Love Lane Farm, now called Red House Farm, reached from Easby Abbey by what is still called Love Lane, but is now a track. Until the mid-eighteenth century it was the main road between Richmond and Brompton-on-Swale, and thence to Catterick and the Great North Road.

Just beyond the farmhouse, on the banks of the river Swale, was a beauty spot, beside an area of broken water which was considered very attractive to Georgian taste. The Richmond schoolmaster and scholar James Tate referred to 'P. Beautement's Foss' in a somewhat pretentious journal he wrote on a sentimental visit to Easby in September 1791 before returning to Cambridge where he was an undergraduate:

> *The fall itself is not high nor extraordinary. Above that for a hundred yards the water runs down a channel, or rather channels of solid rock over whose ridgy inequalities, when the Swale rolls his rain-swollen streams, the impetuosity of the water in conjunction with the roar and foam, present a fine scene.*

The Diarist and her friends often walked out from Richmond to this pleasant destination, sometimes taking tea there. She mainly spells the family's difficult name 'Beautyment', or occasionally 'Beautiment', though the Easby parish registers are consistent in spelling it 'Butement'. The Diarist makes eight references to

Betty Beautyment who, as a farmer, regularly visited Richmond's Saturday market. Indeed the Diarist paid her 7s 6d for butter on 28 December 1766, when butter was doubtless in short supply in the depths of winter, as the cows would be giving little milk and demand was high around Christmas.

Betty had close links with the town, being described as 'of Richmond', when, as Elizabeth Lofthouse, she had married Joseph Butement in Easby Church on 13 January 1737. She and Joseph had four sons and a daughter baptised there between 1737 and 1750. Joseph died in 1755, and Betty continued living as a widow with her family at the farm.

The daughter, Elspith, 'E' or 'Eppey' to the Diarist, was born in 1744 and thus aged 20 when the diary begins; it was noted that 'she is lately marry'd' in May 1765, when she would have been just 21. One of the sons, whose name is not given, transported the Diarist to Winston one Sunday in late June 1765, getting her there in time for the morning service.

Betty Beautyment is one of the few visitors who dined with the Diarist and her Mama. Like Bridget and Hannah Mawer, the Diarist and her Mama were friendly respectively with Elspith and Betty Beautyment. Betty died aged 75 in 1786, so she was about 53 in 1764.

Matty Beauly

Matty (Martha) Beauly/Bewlay/Bewley was another widow who was in business in Richmond, running the King's Arms inn in the market place, where King Street is now, from at least 1741 to 1768. That she was a respected innkeeper is suggested by the purchase from her by the parish church of wine for the Easter communion. She was close to the Diarist, who took tea with her, and she came in to the Diarist's for tea, sometimes with one of the Mawers. On several occasions the Diarist records that she called at Matty's while in the town centre.

The Emersons also knew Matty, and a servant of theirs took her some 'moorgame' on 31 August 1764, presumably as food for the inn to serve. The Diarist supplied her with strawberries on two occasions in July 1765, doubtless for the same purpose. Matty was ill during the hot summer of 1765 and was eventually diagnosed with jaundice. The Diarist was attentive to her during her illness and went to sit with her.

Matty's age is unclear. Although a widow she may not have been elderly, as she was apparently of working age. Martha, widow of Thomas Bewlay of Richmond, was buried at Easby on 27 June 1785, so perhaps there was a connection with the Smiths, or like so many characters in 'The Richmond Diary', maybe she came from Teesdale. There are no records of Beaulys in the Richmond parish registers, and her husband's family may have had links with Darlington. She seems not to have had children.

The Yorke Family

Several generations of the York/Yorke family lived on The Green in Richmond, and represented the town in parliament. Around their mansion they created landscaped gardens which were one of the main sights to see in Georgian Richmond. These were opened to paying visitors on certain Sundays in summer, and on several such occasions the Diarist, with one or more friends, enjoyed a walk in 'Mr York's garden'.

The owner of the estate in the 1760s was Thomas Yorke (1688–1770) who had inherited it from his childless older brother John on the latter's death in 1757. Thomas's wife Abigail had died giving birth to their youngest child in 1741, and his sister-in-law Anne, John's widow, helped bring up his children. Thomas was mainly based in London, and his children were friendly with King George II's young family there.

Thomas's eldest son John, who would later succeed him, married Sophia Glynne of Wales in 1763, and they took over the Richmond estate. Thomas stayed in London. John and Sophia only had one child, a daughter Sophia Anne, who sadly died in infancy, and whose burial in the family vault is mentioned by the Diarist. John took his distraught wife on a cruise to Portugal, but Sophia died on the ship in 1766, shortly after the diary ends. He eventually remarried in 1769, but he and his second wife did not have children.

It would seem that the Diarist or her relations had some link with the Yorke family, for in January 1765, only a couple of days after she had returned from a two-month stay with her aunt and uncle and cousins in Winston, the Diarist walked down to The Green 'to deliver a picture to Mrs York that I brought from Winston'. It would be interesting to know if this was the long-widowed Anne, by now in her early seventies, or the young mother of a baby, Sophia. Bridget Mawer also had a link with the Yorke family, as she was on sufficiently close terms with them to stay at their mansion on The Green in Richmond. The Yorke family, being landowners and members of parliament, were the highest up the social scale of people in the Diarist's circle.

Who is the Diarist?

As must be the case in a diary, the Diarist implicitly makes an appearance in every entry. But by the final entry on Thursday, 16 January 1766, and despite the information provided on her relatives, friends and doings, the identity of this Diarist – her name, her age, her relationships, be she widow, wife or spinster – is as mysterious as when she wrote her first entry on Tuesday, 24 July 1764. So with all the information given by 'The Richmond Diary' and all the evidence assembled by the authors of *Life in Georgian Richmond, North Yorkshire*, who is the Diarist?

As has been apparent from the start, this Diarist is a woman who lives in Richmond in north Yorkshire; she has resided there long enough to be well known by citizens of the most varied classes, and to take advantage of what the town has to offer.

Given her daily pattern of life, as visitor and conversationalist, and her frequent comings and goings among her friends, she must be living among them. If not a house owner, certainly a householder, and – like her neighbours – living in rented accommodation. Yet there is space enough to provide lodgings for herself, her maid, and when necessary, for her Mama and sister, and her Winston relations when they come for the annual races and related celebrations. Also, she is living in accommodation which she can leave for some two months when she goes to stay with her Winston cousins, and to which she may return. Obviously she is not well off by our standards, but she feeds her household, pays her rent, buys clothes and goes to amusements.

All of which suggests that not only is she living in the centre of Richmond, but that she has more space for herself than is enjoyed by many of her friends. She has access to a garden, can put up her visitors, and has enough room for washing, ironing, sewing and other domestic work. The more one follows her life pattern, the more the possibility grows that she must live in somewhere like Bowes Hall, that rambling house described in some detail in a survey of Richmond in 1760 as 'Bowes's House or Hall with a garden on the west and back part thereof containing by estimation one acre'. The Bowes Hall complex of buildings and gardens had been among the properties sold by the trustees of Thomas, Marquess of Wharton, to Sir Conyers D'Arcy in 1729, and purchased by Sir Lawrence Dundas not long before the date of 'The Richmond Diary'.

If this was where she lived, then she would be on the lower reaches of Frenchgate, one of the main streets leading into the town, and the main entrance to Richmond, down which all traffic from the north and east passed. It was also very close to the parish church, set back from the opposite side of the road, which she usually attended twice every Sunday. The site of Bowes Hall today is near Dundas Street, but that thoroughfare was a nineteenth-century improvement to Richmond's circulation pattern, and in the 1760s the Diarist would emerge onto Frenchgate itself.

Confirmation of this Frenchgate location comes from the Diarist when she admits to her special passion – shopping. Invariably she records how she goes 'down' the street to the shops – and with what frequency she will take visitors on shopping expeditions – though she also takes them to church. She even takes orders for ribbons etc. from her Winston cousins – turn right from Bowes Hall and she is outside those shops.

The Diarist's relationship to her Winston cousins – Elizabeth, Isabel, Jane and Frances – becomes very important in the search for her identity. As the Smith family tree shows so clearly, the writer of 'The Richmond Diary' undoubtedly has to be a member of the Smith family which had many links with Easby. A Smith had married into the Emerson family of County Durham, hence the Diarist having an uncle Smith and Emerson cousins. Detailed study of the two families leads to the conclusion that she was the daughter of William Smith and his wife Frances Proud, who had a son Layton and two daughters, Frances and Elizabeth.

The baptisms of these three children have not yet been traced, though they were probably born in London. It seems reasonable to assume that by the mid-1760s they were in their early forties. Of the two daughters, Frances is the most likely candidate for being the Diarist. Frances certainly continued to live in Richmond after the period of 'The Richmond Diary', and married a Richmond grocer, Robert Robson, on 1 April 1769. Both parties were then living in the town, and the marriage was by licence, implying some middle-class pretensions. The bequest under her uncle Thomas Smith's will, drawn up a few months after this marriage, was worded 'I give and devise to my Niece Frances the wife of Robert Robson the sum of five hundred pounds'. 'Mr Robert Robson of Richmond' was buried at Easby on 19 March 1781, and 'Mrs Frances Robson from Richmond widow' was buried there on 3 December 1799.

The Smiths were a family of clerics and academics, so it is not surprising that the Diarist is a well-educated and methodical woman, as well as someone au fait with with fashionable ladylike activities. There are, however, no indications of how or where that education might have been gained. The family had links with London, but her references to the capital give no hints of her direct knowledge of it. Might she be so close to her Emerson cousins because she had grown up with them, and perhaps shared their home studies under their father, the Oxford-educated Revd John Emerson? Against this theory is the fact that the Diarist would seem to have been about ten years older than her Emerson cousins. However, the circle of friends who populate the entries of 'The Richmond Diary' suggest that they had a Teesdale bias.

Towns and Locations

Introduction

First and foremost 'The Richmond Diary' provides invaluable information about life in Richmond in the mid-1760s, where and when it is set, and so the authors have attempted to sketch for readers a pen portrait of what the town was like then. This is followed by briefer outlines of two other, smaller, settlements which are important in the Diarist's story, Easby and Winston. What has come as a surprise to the authors is the extent to which the Diarist, and her circle in and around Richmond, had significant links with London, and so this too is included in this section. That those living in a provincial town should be so familiar with what is happening in the capital at this point in the mid-1760s is a revelation, and reflects how communications were improving.

The university cities of Oxford and Cambridge also weave in and out of the diary, mainly implicitly through the backgrounds of the Smith and Emerson families. A high proportion of graduates entered the Church of England in Georgian times. Clerics in the Allen and Mawer families were more closely linked with Cambridge. Many northern schools had a scholarship link with a Cambridge college. The Revd Francis Blackburne, rector of Richmond at the time of the diary, was a Cambridge man, as was Revd Anthony Temple, Master of the Grammar School. One of Temple's earliest university successes was the Diarist's visitor Revd Christopher Nichols, who was a curate in Cambridge at the time of the diary.

York, the 'Capital of the North', is mentioned occasionally, seemingly mainly as a place people headed for before travelling on elsewhere. The city must, however, also have had a special place in the heart of Mrs Mawer, for it was where, in York Minster, she had married Revd John Mawer.

Richmond

Mid-1760s Richmond was, relatively speaking, a large town, growing and prosperous, attracting new upwardly-mobile residents to enjoy its scenic beauty and fashionable social activities. The single came to seek marriage partners, widows to enjoy congenial cultivated company, and ambitious young men for the trading opportunities. Other 'incomers' included those who came to work for such classes, either as their servants, or as craftspeople supplying them with luxury goods.

Such population growth required more housing. During the Georgian period many existing properties, especially in the ancient cobbled streets of Newbiggin and Frenchgate, were rebuilt as fashionable town houses. These typically not only had handsome symmetrical elevations, but also pleasing interiors, and each room had its own fireplace. Smaller cottages were also built in yards behind the old buildings, and on previously open spaces. There was little outward expansion of the town; the additional capacity was achieved by greater density.

Although the Diarist fails to tell us where she lived, as previously mentioned, there seems no doubt it was in the Frenchgate area, near the parish church, and where the market place shops would be 'down Street'. Even today, Frenchgate has a mixed streetscape of Georgian town houses and smaller cottages, but in the 1760s it would have retained a number of older buildings dating back to medieval times, some of them timber-framed, and many of them only one-and-a-half storeys high. These typically had a multi-function ground-floor living and sleeping room with a large fireplace to provide heating and cooking facilities, plus some artificial light, and an unheated room above used for additional sleeping.

The Georgian rebuilding, which took place over a long period, saw some of the older cottages amalgamated into a single, larger, property. Sometimes there was not a complete rebuilding, but instead a smart new facade was added onto an older structure. The gracious accommodation provided by these fashionable town houses was often rented by those unable to own a house themselves.

Careful study of the comings and goings of the Diarist's closest friends indicates that they were all living in very close proximity, possibly all tenanting apartments within Bowes Hall, the large complex formerly set back from the west side of Frenchgate just above Dundas Street. James Readhead is recorded as the main tenant of the building, and William Morgetroy was a market gardener cultivating its large garden.

Bowes Hall was named from its former owners for many centuries, the Richmond branch of the distinguished northern family of Bowes, several of whom had represented the town in parliament. From about 1727 it was rented out, and eventually demolished about 1785. In 1820 a writer recorded:

> *Some of the old inhabitants recollect a very large room upon the first landing, with five windows, two facing the north and two the south, with one towards the east, the compartments of which were filled with escutcheons painted on the glass, the figures very boldly executed. The ground floor consisted of offices and a very large kitchen.*

This description fits a medieval form with the main living accommodation above the ground level. The combination of faded grandeur and low rents due to some dilapidation is likely to have appealed to the Diarist and possibly several of her friends, maybe even including the more prosperous Mawers. There might also have been sufficient space for the Wilsons' school. Who occupied which part, including the large main room on the first-floor with its heraldic glass, is an intriguing conundrum!

Richmond's street pattern in the 1760s was still constrained by the medieval defensive wall built about 1311 around the market place or bailey, with only two gateways in it for vehicular traffic, at the bottom of Frenchgate and in Finkle Street. Both of these would be removed about 1774 to improve traffic flow, but the Diarist probably passed through the tumbledown remains of Frenchgate Bar every time she went 'down Street' into the town centre. Later in the Georgian period new roads would be created to improve access into the market place – New Road coming up from the bridge in 1772, and King Street leading in from the north in 1812.

Easby

Not only is the Diarist from a family which had in earlier generations been closely linked with the nearby village of Easby, but a large number of the characters who occur in its pages also had links with Easby. It would seem that these ancient ties, of who had known whom in the past, were of great importance in the 1760s.

Easby lies immediately adjacent to the eastern boundary of Richmond. Pleasant woodland and riverside walks to Easby from Richmond were popular in Georgian times as now. The ecclesiastical parish of Easby is, and was, a very large rural area, although the village itself is very small. On a few occasions the Diarist and her friends walked beyond Easby along Love Lane to the farmhouse which was the home of her friend Betty Beautyment.

The Smiths, the Diarist's family, had significant links with Easby and owned property there, including the impressive ruins of Easby Abbey, although she does not mention these. Many of the Smith family, having left the parish to spend their careers elsewhere, returned in later life and were then buried at Easby, including the Diarist.

Several of the lesser characters who pop up in the pages of the diary seem also to have had links with Easby. Some Richmond people of the genteel class with whom the Diarist mixed also deliberately moved out of Richmond to Easby, such as John and Elizabeth Close, who moved to Easby House, a Smith property, in April 1765. Many of the other characters in 'The Richmond Diary' also had some link with Easby, such as the mysterious Matthew Graham who was eventually buried there at the age of 86 in 1805.

Winston

The Diarist's links with the village of Winston in Teesdale were clearly also very strong, although only going back a single generation. The aunt, uncle, and cousins there, played a huge part in her life, so much so that the authors have wondered if she had grown up with them, although that is still unclear. Doubtless many people even today would regard close family links as a major part of their lives. However, several other characters who feature in her story, and that of Richmond, also have their origins in Teesdale, such as the Cornforths, who lived in the hamlet of Barforth, just across the river Tees from Winston, within the parish of Forcett, where all were buried.

At the east end of the pleasant village of Winston, on the north bank of the river Tees about twelve miles northwest of Richmond, is its parish church. Next to the church is the former rectory, a large rambling and typically Georgian parsonage, which at the time of 'The Richmond Diary' was the home of the Emerson family. Here lived the Diarist's paternal aunt, Ann, the wife of the rector, and their four daughters, her cousins. The Diarist refers to the Winston rectory as 'home', which may imply she had lived there earlier. The rectory must have had an orchard – from which the Diarist was sent apples and pears.

Journeys between Richmond and Winston by the Diarist, the Emersons, and their servants, had recently been greatly facilitated by the construction from 1761 of a turnpike road from Staindrop running southwards towards Gilling West, just north of Richmond. The turnpike road crossed the river Tees at Winston by a handsome new bridge constructed shortly before 'The Richmond Diary' begins. This much-improved route must have been of great importance to the Emersons and the Diarist, who only a few years earlier would, if travelling between Richmond and Winston, have had either to cross the treacherous river Tees by a ford at Winston, or make much longer trips via bridges at either Barnard Castle or Piercebridge.

If the Diarist did live at Winston earlier in her life, this turnpike road might have been a determining factor in her decision to move to Richmond to take advantage of the more sophisticated lifestyle available there. She certainly maintained close links with many Teesdale people other than the Emersons.

London

The Diarist shows that the sophistication of London was being observed in Richmond, despite it taking coaches several days to get there. Long hours spent sharing such journeys brought together a wide mix of people. Did news reach the Diarist's Richmond circle, which clearly was interested in musical performances, of the 8-year-old Wolfgang Amadeus Mozart? His breathtakingly prodigious concerts took by storm society in London, then the wealthiest city in Europe, and his time there coincides almost exactly with 'The Richmond Diary'.

Richmond families were connected to the capital through marriages and the professions. The Diarist had several family members there, including her brother Layton in the Fleet Prison, and his wife Nanny Smith, and children, her nieces Ann and Wilhelmina. The lawyer, uncle Thomas Smith, was permanently based in London, and her eldest cousin Elizabeth Emerson visited the capital. A relative by marriage, William Allen, was based at the court of Queen Charlotte, the young wife of George III, but paid two visits to Richmond in the summer of 1765.

Friends too had links with London. Alice Nicholl lived there, despite spending six months in Richmond during the time covered by 'The Richmond Diary'. Bridget Mawer had an older half-sister, Henrietta Cotesworth, who became a sub-governess in the royal nursery. Bridget was clearly on closer terms with the Yorke family of The Green than was the Diarist, and the children of Thomas Yorke, who was based mainly at Kensington, had been playmates of the young children of George II at Kensington Palace. Old Mrs Metcalfe also had a son working in London.

To save the high cost of postage, letters were sent by people travelling up or down to London from Richmond or Winston. These 'postmen' were not only relatives and close friends, but included people who do not feature otherwise in the diary, such as the maid's brother, and 'young Mr Gail' of Scruton.

Our well-educated Diarist knew from her awareness of London how her daily entries qualified her as a sophisticated recorder of her world. Unbeknown to her, her near contemporary in London, Fanny Burney, was working out her own diary role, in her case writing to Nobody, 'since to Nobody can I be wholly unreserved'.

The Diarist records only one bookshop purchase, that in November 1765 of 'a new Almanack, cost 9d'. Almanacs were among the most popular publications for almost all classes, but 9d – possibly about £6 in 2016 terms – puts her purchase well above the average price. By the 1760s they were becoming more expensive, serving not only as basic reference books, but more like an appointments diary which no sophisticated lady – or diarist – could be without.

Richmond was following London in monitoring tea-drinking and other social gatherings. The dances that the Diarist attends are large even by London standards, and Richmond's theatrical performances, stimulated by London-style presentations, are well supported to the benefit of audiences and actors. London was also sending fashionable consumer merchandise to stock Richmond's shops, inspected regularly not only by the Diarist but also her visitors, who came to window-gaze as well as make purchases. So confidently is Richmond adopting new cultural movements emanating from London, that Mr and Mrs Wilson feel encouraged to develop their school for young ladies – older girls drawn from Richmond and elsewhere – preparing the next generation of home-makers and social organisers.

'The Richmond Diary' and the 1760s

Taking Tea

'The Richmond Diary' provides a vivid picture of what life was like in the mid-1760s. Particularly valuable is the information on many social activities. Background details of these are required to enhance the diary entries themselves.

'Taking Tea' is treated first because it takes up so much of the Diarist's time. It does not refer to the casual 'cuppa' of today, for in the 1760s tea was still a very expensive commodity (around 15s per pound weight). The Diarist's 'taking tea' with her women friends relates to a special ritual which had begun a century before in London, and had been rapidly copied across the country. If Georgian men had their coffee houses for social gatherings, their wives and daughters had the more homely attraction of tea.

The general rules of behaviour for tea taking are well documented, though commentators tend to over-rely on the accounts of aristocratic London ladies. Which is why 'The Richmond Diary' is so valuable for recording the sort of practises that prevailed in the north, away from the capital.

Women regularly assembled in their homes in small groups for the purpose of drinking tea and engaging freely in conversation and gossip. They were there as a consequence of an invitation to attend, or their issue of such invitations. Such sessions would last for anything from one to three hours. According to the Diarist, tea was taken two, or perhaps three or four times in a week, and even sometimes on Sundays, and at around 5.00 pm, never earlier in the day as in the south, perhaps because there were many domestic requirements to be met.

These invitation-only sessions were all-women affairs and were not generally open to husbands or visitors, although Mr Wilson and Dr Pringle were rare exceptions. Two to four women were present, the same individuals appearing regularly. In general Mrs Mawer and the Diarist hosted such sessions, wherever held, perhaps due to the expense and organisation involved, and suitability of surroundings in terms of the room, furniture and household goods.

Such gatherings were recognised ceremonies, so required their own 'equipage' – cups, saucers, teaspoons, teapot and kettle, laid out on a tea table. A small decorative chest stored the precious tea. It was China tea, and taken very weak, it would seem. Delicate cups and saucers, reserved solely for tea gatherings, were ordered from a 'China Shop', and could be of English or foreign origin.

'The Richmond Diary' documents just how central taking tea was to the Diarist and her circle, and how it celebrated women's friendships and activities. This explains why paintings of the time so frequently depicted these tea gatherings, and why the authors of contemporary novels portrayed their characters at tea. Taking tea had become recognised as expressive of a growing age of leisure, and it also provided an opportunity for women to decide how to spend their time.

Conversation

Just as 'Taking Tea' was not the same as enjoying the modern 'cuppa', so 'conversation' was very different from a chat between women today. Obviously the women taking tea, or enjoying a walk or shopping trip together, would talk to each other, but the art of proper conversation was reserved for a special time of day, mainly the evening, when the events of the day could be reflected upon.

The Diarist's daily record of her evening happenings shows how important they were to her and her friends, crucially providing opportunities for women's uninterrupted conversation. They could talk informally among themselves, to demonstrate how polite verbal exchanges took place, and how they cultivated politeness and gentility. There was an important distinction between chat and conversation – as Dr Johnson explained, 'We had talk enough, but no conversation, there was nothing discussed.'

What occupies the evenings takes up much of 'The Richmond Diary'. Almost invariably the Diarist names those whom she has seen after taking tea, or occasionally even after supper, around 9.00 pm, and for how long, before she regularly goes to bed about 10.00 pm. Typical entries run: 'in the Eve Mrs Mawer and Miss came in', 'in the evening we all went to Mrs Mawer's', 'in the Eve Mrs Wilson sat an hour with us'.

When possible, the Diarist arranged to spend her evenings with Mrs and Miss Mawer, or Mrs Wilson. As ladies of significance, they were no doubt well spoken, educated in genteel behaviour, and presumably with sensible views on the people they all knew, and on what was taking place around them. Mr Wilson would occasionally join them, given his role as a professional teacher.

Sometimes Mrs Wilson's 'young ladies' from the school would be present, for example Miss Wycliffe, Miss Carr, Miss Hogg. After all, their syllabus would certainly have included 'manners, deportment, conversation'. Contemporary manuals emphasised how conversation lay at the heart of sociability. By the 1760s women were expected to be capable of socialising, of participating more fully in domestic and social life and, through such newly acquired skills, able to run homes and express their own views and even expectations.

With such expectations, it is not surprising that these evenings could last from half-an-hour to two hours. The Diarist would of course be talking with her friends many times during the day – while visiting, shopping, taking tea – except, it would seem, when out taking longer walks in the countryside, when another sort of more suitable conversation would take over.

By this mid-Georgian period, conversation as a desirable skill had been adopted into other cultured activities. Painters such as Hogarth and Gainsborough, and many lesser artists, were producing 'conversation pieces' representing a much more informal approach to portraiture, showing families or friends in more relaxed poses, in their gardens or drawing rooms.

The vogue for novel reading among the middle class – and visibly influencing the Diarist's writing style – also led to the view that such writers as Richardson, Fielding, and Smollet should be read as conversational aids, especially because so many of their characters and plots are set in London, and so reveal that cosmopolitan world of desirable social behaviour.

'A Very Genteel Meeting' exclaimed the Diarist on 6 September 1764, after exercising her developing social skills and vocabulary at the assembly after the race day.

Letter Writing

As by the mid-eighteenth century correspondence was beginning to be published, so letter writing became a literary genre. An almost exclusively female activity in the 1760s, it is a comment on increasing literacy among women, and formed a fashionable sophistication like polite conversation and the taking of tea.

The Richmond Diarist tabulates her correspondence as carefully as her record of who called and who visited, and the current topics of conversation. Over the period covered by the diary some eighty letters are exchanged, which averages about one a week. Letters in and out are entered, detailing who received mail and who wrote to whom. About a third of the letters are written to the Diarist. Both the reading and writing of letters took up a surprising amount of time. Letters received were read by several people, and often shared with others over tea drinking. Letter writing mainly took place in the mornings.

Even without seeing the letters we can deduce their purpose and aims. Through her correspondence the Diarist administers family connections, maintains relationships – and devotes much of her time to developing her writing craft. Letters not only conveyed current information about family members and absent friends, but sometimes included other news such as what was happening in London and the fashions there.

The greatest number of exchanges are between the Diarist and her sister in Richmond, and their cousins Isabel, Jane and Frances Emerson in Winston, who make arrangements to visit, to see the races, attend the assemblies, and go on shopping sprees. Concerns about health also feature. Another important group of letters are between the Richmond sisters and their relatives, the Smiths, in London.

The Diarist's sister, apparently an enthusiastic scribe, largely received and wrote her letters at the weekends, which may have been when she was resident in Richmond. To a degree, she serves as the secretary of the household and, like the Diarist, is fully aware of what is happening within and around the family. She is on especially close terms with Alice Nichols, away in London for much of the time, and cousin Fanny Emerson in Winston. Mama seems to have typified her older generation by being much less involved with letter writing. She received few letters, probably more of a business than a social nature, and mainly relating to Ann Smith in London.

The importance of letter writing is further demonstrated by how much it must have cost. In addition to paper and ink, postage was very expensive, and slow before the introduction of royal mail coaches. Letters took several days to reach their destination – those between the Diarist and Winston took about four days. It could be a liability to receive letters because the postage was borne by the recipient until the introduction of the penny post in 1840. One letter frequently enclosed another, to save cost. Whenever possible deliveries were made by hand, making use of servants travelling back and forth to Winston for example – and especially people travelling to Richmond from London, bringing mail with them.

Communications

Life in Georgian Richmond, North Yorkshire reflects an age of rapid change in communications. As an increasingly important market

town, Richmond was served by many local carriers bringing people
selling goods from a wide area, as well as those within Swaledale.
Many main roads were being improved under the turnpike system,
facilitating quicker and safer journeys, and coaching services
were increasingly offering reliable public transport between
major centres. Journeys to York, Cambridge and London would
necessitate travelling to Catterick Bridge, the nearest point to
Richmond on the Great North Road, to connect with coaching
services.

The Catterick Bridge road through Brompton-on-Swale had
been improved under the Richmond-Lancaster turnpike road
of 1751, and the town had also been connected to the Tees port
of Yarm by a 1747 turnpike road. Turnpike acts of parliament
transferred the unpopular requirement for parishes to provide
labour to maintain roads, begun in Elizabethan times, to the new
roads. Six days of this 'statute labour' had to be provided by all
householders each year, and parish highways surveyors had to
organise this. To avoid manual work, some householders loaned
carts to help the task, others 'compounded' or paid in lieu of doing
the work themselves, and this went towards hiring carts. Some sent
their servants, or simply dodged and were charged as defaulters.
The only reference to this comes under Wednesday, 20 March
1765 when the Diarist notes 'I paid Christopher Wright a shilling
for a Common Day's work'.

At the time of 'The Richmond Diary', journeys between Winston
and Richmond had recently been made much quicker and easier
by the construction of a turnpike road from Staindrop in County
Durham to what is now the A66. Among the local landowners
backing the scheme were the Diarist's lifelong Teesdale friends, the
Cornforth family. The turnpike included the building of a brand
new bridge across the river Tees at Winston, replacing a ford there,
and this probably explains why it seems to have been such a novelty
for the Emersons and their servants to make frequent journeys to
Richmond, or for the Diarist so easily to visit Winston. Designed
by Sir Thomas Robinson of nearby Rokeby Hall and constructed
1762–3, Winston Bridge's impressive single span of 111ft gave it a
surprise role in the 1988 TV series *Piece of Cake* when Squadron
Leader Ray Hanna, a former Red Arrows pilot, flew a spitfire under
it, the stunt having only 2ft clearance above the river.

The Diarist mostly travelled on foot in and around Richmond,
but occasionally she rode in a chaise, a light two-wheeled vehicle
drawn by one horse. Such a ride was a special treat and worthy
of record, probably because she was lucky enough to get a lift if

someone else was paying for it. When Mama was invited to a tea
party at Dr Pringle's in October 1764, Mrs James, who seems to
have been a stranger on a brief stay in Richmond, sent her chaise
for 'us', and the Diarist went in a chaise to the dancing school ball
in December 1765 with two pupils from the Wilsons' school. Her
cousin Fanny Emerson went up to the racecourse in Mr Witham's
coach, a much grander experience than anything that seems to
have happened to the Diarist. One must assume that there were
sedan chairs available for hire in Richmond at this time, but there
is no suggestion that even Mama used such – perhaps they were
too expensive.

The Diarist's Clothing

Most of the Diarist's many references to shopping, or, by implication,
window shopping, relate to clothes and their components and
accessories. When she has bought, rather than browsed, she records
her purchases, usually noting the amount spent. Before the days of
ready-made clothing, the items usually had to be made up for her
by the shop, and the yardage of material is noted. Some references
relate to her making items of clothing herself, and some purchases
probably relate to domestic material. Individual clothing items
warrant a capital letter, e.g. Gown, Apron, Ruffles.

The Diarist rarely buys a major garment. There are just two
references to 'gowns'. She bought a new one of 'stuff' (a type of
fairly utilitarian woollen cloth), the fabric for which was purchased
at 1s 3d per yard, and got her Mama a more expensive one costing
2s 1d per yard. This was of 'poplin', a cloth made using a silk warp
and a fine worsted weft. Petticoats, not then undergarments, were
important. In June 1765 the Diarist treated herself to a black
'shallon' (fine wool) petticoat at 1s 9d per yard.

The garments mentioned most frequently are aprons of different
sorts. A checked apron for household work, as in the modern sense
of the word, was purchased for 9d, whereas 1½yd of plain gauze
costing the large sum of 3s 6d per yard was to make a delicate apron
as an over-garment. The reference to 'drawing ruffles' is to a similar
decorative accoutrement, which took several weeks to make. A
flowered lawn apron and ruffles were raffled, and Bell Emerson was
the lucky winner of the first prize, the flowered lawn apron.

Handkerchiefs were a fashion accessory, and as usual the
Diarist spent more on some for Mama than herself. Mama's silk
handkerchief cost 4s 6d, whereas on the same trip a pair of shoes
and a pocket handkerchief for herself came to only 2s 9d; a black

handkerchief for the Diarist cost 5s. On Christmas Eve 1765, Mama was bought three pocket-handkerchiefs. Ribbons (called ribbands) for decorating dresses or perhaps straw hats, were purchased more than once to send to her cousins at Winston.

Headgear features infrequently. The Diarist bought a new hat, possibly a summer bonnet, costing 4s 5d (something which could be bought 'off the shelf') and she made herself a 'nett' hood. One of the pupils at the Wilsons' school, Miss Wycliffe, came into the house for the Diarist to teach her to 'nett', a Georgian practice of women making net material for various domestic and personal purposes, in this case probably a hair covering. One surprising entry is a payment to Mr Watson of 8s for a 'tupee', presumably a toupee, not the modern device for hiding a bald patch, but a raised roll of hair worn just above the forehead, over which both men and women combed their front hair to form a topknot. The Diarist also alludes to a peruke maker in the town, John Maxwell, of whose work she presumably knew.

Stays were a vital piece of Georgian underclothing, and the staymaker was an important craftsman in Georgian Richmond – the Diarist paid Mr Jackson £1 5s for his handiwork. Special entries regarding clothing record the white hoods, scarves and gloves worn when the Diarist acted as a pallbearer at two funerals.

Other people's clothing is also mentioned. Bridget Mawer, who was probably much better off than the Diarist, got Mrs Storey to make her a new 'neglejay', a loose informal gown rather than the light dressing gown version of the modern negligee. This is the only reference to a named person making clothes. A letter to the Diarist's sister enclosed some patterns intended for Miss Mawer, these are likely to have been small samples of fashionable dress fabrics.

As well as expensive handkerchiefs, the Diarist provided her Mama with shifts, which she made, and white worsted stockings, which she presumably knitted. The Diarist spent a great many hours spinning, possibly to produce knitting yarn. The half-ounce of cotton purchased for her aunt at Winston may have been for lacemaking.

Purchases of cloth, seemingly for domestic use, include 6yd of diaper, possibly for napery, which were sent to Winston. Was the 6lb of 'lint' purchased from the Quaker merchant James Masterman actually linen cloth, perhaps for bed linen?

Shops & Shopkeepers

The Diarist and her friends and cousins clearly enjoyed the shops – they are given a capital letter in the text – and almost ten per cent of the diary entries refer directly to, or allude to, shopping. In the mid-1760s, shops in the modern sense were a relatively new phenomenon and Richmond, as a very up-to-date and relatively large and prosperous town, had shops which people from other places envied. Indeed, the number of shops in the market place had been increased from the 1740s by the corporation building a large freestanding Toll Booth and encouraging the construction of premises in the central island around the medieval Trinity chapel.

The traditional guild crafts were well represented in the Diarist's Richmond – grocers, drapers, tailors, shoemakers, and carpenters who could 'up their game' to become cabinetmakers producing elegant, fashionable furniture. The corporation's positive encouragement of additional skills noted by Samuel and Nathaniel Buck meant that there were also clockmakers, upholsterers, picture-framers, cutlers, staymakers, even hairdressers and – a rare luxury – a bookseller. Run from at least 1737 by John Raine, and from his death in 1764 by Isabella 'Tibby' Tinkler, a highly knowledgeable shopkeeper, the Finkle Street bookseller would supply the Diarist with her writing paper, almanacs, and perhaps also music books. No wonder people flocked to Richmond from a wide area less well served by such shopping expertise, and it is significant that on several occasions the Diarist notes that she went shopping for something requested by her Winston relatives.

The Diarist and her circle clearly greatly enjoyed outings 'down Street' to the shops in and around the market place. About a quarter of her references to such visits indicate that she went with other people, mainly the Emerson cousins, but sometimes Bridget Mawer, suggesting that it was a social as well as a commercial activity. Her main shopping day was Saturday, the market day, although Tuesdays and Thursdays were also popular. Shopping usually took place quite late in the day, not only after dinner, but sometimes after tea, and even into the evening on a Fair Day (6 July 1765). Many of the visits seem to have been for 'window shopping', as the Diarist records when she has made purchases. Drapers' and haberdashers' shops unsurprisingly seem to have been of the most significance to the Diarist, most of which were run by women for women.

The Diarist's closest association was with Miss Faith Dixon, who had a drapery shop on the high row, where Warne's grocers is now. She lived on the premises, her home having a separate entrance from a passage at the side of the shop. Miss Dixon was of a highly respectable Richmond family, her brother, William, having been town clerk, and at the time of 'The Richmond Diary' she was a middle-aged spinster. Part way through the document the Diarist changes from referring to her as 'Miss Dixon', to 'Mrs Dixon' or 'Mrs F Dixon', possibly as a mark of respect for her age, as the Diarist tends to use the term 'Miss' for young women.

As a good customer, the Diarist had an account at Faith Dixon's shop, settling up in February and October 1765. She was on tea-drinking terms with her, at the houses of both of them, and on one occasion walked to Easby with Faith to see Mrs Close, who had recently moved there from Richmond. Another draper's shop was run by Miss Jane Wrather, who organised a lottery which unfortunately did not comply with legislation, and she was hauled before the Borough Quarter Sessions. Yet another draper was Miss Wayd.

In a slightly more superior league socially and economically was Thomas Simpson, who, as a mercer, sold superior dress fabrics, and also owned several properties in the town. Again the Diarist was on social terms with his wife, and visited her to see their new baby as well as to drink tea.

One of the few references to a shop for anything other than clothing or food is the entry 'down at the China Shop in the morning' on Monday, 27 August 1764. Presumably this visit was to purchase more of the refined equipment required for the important social activity of tea drinking, and it is the only reference to shopping before dinner or tea.

Expenditure on non-clothing items

The Diarist's 'down street' activities seem generally not to relate to buying food. Obviously this must have taken place, presumably mainly in the Saturday market, but food is only occasionally mentioned apropos prices. It is likely that the town's many 'shops', where people went to select merchandise, sold non-food items. How the Diarist obtained her tea is particularly intriguing!

'The Richmond Diary' contains miscellaneous scraps of information on her expenditure. The purpose of these is unclear, as they cannot record all her outgoings. Perhaps some are intended to tell us something was expensive, or increasing in price, or maybe that the Diarist felt she had got a bargain. She seems to have been in charge of expenditure for her household, paying the rent and for coal, and may have been recording what she was learning about running a Georgian household with a view to a hoped-for future marriage.

It seems to be implicit that there was little money to spend, which fits with the inference that she was the daughter of an impoverished and widowed mother. Early on in the diary (Saturday, 26 January 1765) is the entry 'Mr Bently paid us 15s for Layton's books and returned them he could not dispose of', suggesting the family was trying to raise money by selling things it no longer needed. Further evidence of financial difficulty is suggested by the entry on Friday, 19 July 1765: 'Paid Mrs Readhead the half year's rent due Mayday £5 0s 0d', so the rent was more than two months overdue.

The Diarist got in six loads of coal at 10d each in late February 1765, paying a week later, and in early April another ten loads at the slightly dearer price of 10½d. This was a period when Georgian town houses were being fitted with a fireplace in each room, and impoverished widows might choose to live in Richmond because its proximity to County Durham's pits made its coal relatively cheap. It appears that in the Diarist's household, Mama's room was kept warmer than others, which might fit with their abode being Bowes Hall, an old-fashioned house still with few rooms suitable for a fire. Or maybe the price of coal gave the Diarist as much anxiety as a large gas bill might give us today.

People engaging in social activities such as entertaining guests in the evening needed many candles, as oil was not yet being used for lamps. Mama had some link, possibly a family connection, with a Mr Robinson in Barnard Castle, writing to order some candles in the dark days of November 1765, and sending 16s for the previous lot. He sent three dozen at 19s just before that Christmas.

On Saturday, 20 September 1764 the Diarist gives us a résumé of the prices of several food items in Richmond market that day. Wheat was 6s 6d a bushel, beef and mutton 3d/lb, and a loin of veal much more expensive at 4s. Meat was sold only in the butchers' shambles, a ramshackle timber-framed building in the market place, but at the time of the diary an improved shambles was being constructed by the corporation on the south side where the market hall is today. The Diarist paid one of the Richmond millers for corn £3 5s 3d on 13 April 1765, presumably for about 10 bushels. In February 1765 butter was 10d/lb, but by Christmas it had gone up to 11d, and Betty Beautyment was paid 7s 6d for the commodity just after Christmas, presumably a sum owed for butter supplied over that period.

Social Activities

Life in Georgian Richmond, North Yorkshire is an invaluable source of information about the many Georgian leisure pursuits fashionable at a time when the town was becoming a leading provincial centre. The most prestigious was the assembly, a formal gathering of members of polite society under the direction of a Master of Ceremonies. Younger people, seeking potential marriage partners, danced under the watchful eyes of those of an older generation who could occupy themselves with card games.

Richmond corporation had recently built a handsome assembly room, then as now, called the town hall, where the Diarist attended several functions. The most important assemblies were those held on the evenings of the races, and the Diarist attended all three in September 1764, giving details of how many couples danced and how late she returned home. She was too ill to attend the following year, but her Emerson cousins provided her with the statistics for her journal.

Slightly less prestigious events, referred to as balls, were held later in the Richmond season. The Diarist was well enough to attend again by the October of 1765 – 'We danced 20 couples' – and to celebrate the election of each year's mayor on St Hilary's Day (13 January). The Diarist knew from her youth the new young mayor for 1765, Thomas Cornforth, and enjoyed the ball he held on 21 January to celebrate his taking office – 'we danced 26 couples … home at 2'.

Each year a visiting dancing master set up a school to teach people the latest intricate dances, as detailed by 'The Richmond Diary'. The master in 1765 – a man called Nichol – began his classes late in the July ahead of the autumn season, and by 15 August his pupils were sufficiently rehearsed for the Diarist to report, 'went to Dancing School to see the children dance'. It is unclear whether the 'children' included any of the young ladies at the school run by Mr and Mrs Wilson, with which the Diarist was involved.

The dancing school continued right through to the Christmas season. The Diarist made three further visits in September, and again on 8 November: 'it being a public night', and also on 12 December. The last reference to Mr Nichol's work is 30 December: 'The Dancing School ball. I went in the chaise…'. A ride in a horse-drawn vehicle gave the Diarist great excitement. Her account of the first day of the 1764 races – Tuesday, 4 September – includes the note that her youngest cousin, Fanny Emerson, rode on the 'Moor' in Mr Witham's coach!

The Richmond social season of assemblies, horse races and plays was timed to coincide with the annual muster of the Richmond-based North York Militia, the officers of which, in their impressive red uniforms, were a star attraction of the assemblies. The entry for

Monday, 27 May 1765 mentions that the militia was coming into town for a month. Doubtless they were back again when, on 24 July 1765, she visited Rosa Pringle, who had that January become the second wife of the Roman Catholic doctor Dr James Pringle, a close family friend, and the two women then went to a concert at the town hall – 'We subscribed 1s 6d for one night'.

Although the details of this concert are not given, we know that there were many musicians in Richmond around this time. The travelling players visiting that summer may also have been sufficiently talented as musicians to give concerts. The town had an official liveried band of waits, employed to provide entertainment at public functions, and they probably played for dancing at the assemblies. Even the Diarist's stay-maker, Robert Jackson, could entertain a social gathering by playing his violin.

Richmond also had an important link with Sir William Herschel, more famous as an astronomer, but earlier in his career a distinguished musician. He had begun as a player of the hautboy, a type of oboe fashionable in early Georgian times, and violinist in the Hanoverian Guard, and then been recruited to train the bands of northern militias, including those of Durham and Richmondshire. Patronised by Ralph, 5th baronet Milbank, who, with his wife Elizabeth, was a keen amateur musician, Herschel published music including two Richmond symphonies.

Walking in pleasure gardens and along scenic routes was an important part of Georgian social life, and the Diarist makes many references to this. On 5 August 1764 she walked in 'Mr York's garden' – the famous gardens created by successive generations of the Yorke family around their mansion on The Green. On 15 August she walked 'round the Castle', which is likely to mean along the Castle Walk, created as a Georgian Promenade in the early eighteenth century. There are also references to walking to Easby, and from there along Love Lane to the farm where there was a beauty spot on the River Swale, and on Friday, 21 October she 'walk'd to Ask(e) Wood', presumably to admire the autumnal colours.

A rather more populist event mentioned is the Fair Day on Tuesday, 25 September 1765, during the annual Rood Fair. She calls the previous day the 'Beast Fair', because this was primarily for cattle sales, but there would also be a lot of stalls selling a great variety of wares. Doubtless there were entertainers, in addition to those noted by the Diarist as amusing the market-day crowds some Saturdays in summer 1764.

The Races

Richmond has been linked with the 'Sport of Kings' – and indeed queens – since the time of the first Queen Elizabeth. Queen Anne presented several gold cups to the Richmond horse races throughout her reign. During the eighteenth century horseracing became a highly fashionable leisure activity for the wealthier echelons of society, who carefully bred and trained horses as well as attending races.

The races became one of the highlights of Richmond's social calendar and, being on a par with those of York and Doncaster, some of the best horses ran here. Racehorse training remained an important part of the town's economic life until the late twentieth century, when townsfolk still took an immense interest in racing news. 'The Richmond Diary' amply illustrates that news of which horses won which races formed a vital topic of conversation over the teacups in the mid-1760s, even among those people who were able only to attend the races, rather than entering runners themselves.

'The Richmond Diary' covers two race meetings, during the first week of September in both 1764 and 1765. The Richmond races were held for three days, on the Wednesday, Thursday and Friday, with a number of races being run each day. The actual races were not like present-day races, but consisted of a heat, or heats, over perhaps three miles, with a run-off between the fastest two horses. On top of this the horses were of course walked from their home to Richmond, and then ran the heats, and if successful the race, and then walked home again, so they had to be much more robust animals than modern racehorses.

The Diarist, doubtless having heard much talk in the town of the winning horses, carefully noted their names. She would know, or know of, some of the owners. For 1764 she recorded that the race on 'Wednesday 5th' with the biggest purse, 'the £50', was won by 'Whitworth', the bay colt belong to Mr John Hutton, the much-respected squire of Marske in Swaledale. For 'Thursday 6th', her journal records a particularly significant event in racing history, that the Gold Cup was won by his horse 'Silvio'.

The Gold Cup, established by the corporation in 1759, was the most important of the Richmond races. For the first five years of its existence, the Gold Cup had been won by the Duke of Cleveland's 'Dainty Davy', and four times 'Silvio' had been second, but in 1764, 'Silvio' won. The jockey was Charles Dawson, who then retired and set up as a trainer in Richmond, building a house still called 'Silvio House'. The Diarist, aware of the high drama of that day, celebrated – 'All at the Assembly, all danced. A very genteel meeting'. The following day she went to see the trophy itself, at Mrs Bowes's, where it was presumably on display.

The highly-prized trophy was retained by the owner of that year's winning horse, and each year the corporation commissioned a new piece of silver-gilt plate from leading London silversmiths, such as Daniel Smith and Robert Sharp, at a cost of about £80. The 1764 cup was the first of several made to a design commissioned by Thomas Dundas, son of Sir Lawrence Dundas of Aske Hall, from the famous Scottish architect Robert Adam.

Incredibly, 'The Richmond Diary' covers a pivotal change in the history of the Richmond races. Those held in 1764 were the last to be held on the old informal racecourse on the High Moor, where the track had to be defined with tapes each year. Those held in 1765 were the first to be run on the new permanent racecourse laid out on Whitcliffe Pasture, a move which enhanced the status of the Richmond races. Ten years later an elegant grandstand would be built on the new site designed by the architect John Carr of York, who also designed grandstands for York and Doncaster racecourses.

The Diarist again recorded the highlights of all three race days in 1765. The winner of the £50 race at the end of the Tuesday was of particular significance to her, for it was 'Dido', owned by William Cornforth, who was based at Barford Hall Stud near Gainford, and related to her friend Thomas Cornforth, the mayor of Richmond that year. Two of her Emerson cousins, Bell and Fanny, were staying with her for the races, both were at the assemblies held on the Tuesday and Wednesday evenings, and 'both danced' at the assembly after the Gold Cup on the Thursday.

The importance of the races to the Diarist and her circle is reflected in the amount of effort put into preparing her home beforehand, with several days spent cleaning in anticipation of the many visitors expected. This was the only event when the house party included male guests as well as Emerson cousins. Not everyone was keen on the races – Mrs Mawer clearly left Richmond to avoid them, though returned immediately they were over, and it seems likely that Mama also was elsewhere.

It was expensive for the mayor and corporation to put on the races, and sponsorship for the various prizes was raised from among the wealthy horse-owners who would compete, local innholders who did valuable trade during the races, and other local businesspeople. Two gentlemen, usually from the landowning fraternity, were appointed stewards for each year, and they oversaw the running of the actual races, as today. The corporation staff had to deal with the entries for the races, usually submitted by a servant of the horse's owner, giving its name, whether male or female, colour, age, and pedigree, for the purpose of betting. A typical example is the entry by Askrigg trainer John Pratt in 1778 – 'I name for the 3 year old filly's subscription next year at Richmond a bay filly got by Syphon out of Tincalo's dam'.

By the time the 1765 Richmond races were held, preparations were already in hand for those of the following year. A newspaper advertisement in the *Newcastle Courant* in October 1765 announced the rules and prize for a race on Gold Cup day the following year.

> *We, whose Names are here-under written, do agree to run each a Colt or Filly, one Three mile Heat, over Richmond Race, in 1766, the same Day the Cup is run for, for Twenty Guineas each, Play or Pay; the Colts to carry eight Stone seven Pounds; the Fillies, eight Stone five Pounds each. The Subscribers to send the Marks and Pedigree of each Colt or Filly to the Mayor of Richmond, on or before the first Day of December next, and none but Subscribers, at that Time, to be allowed to enter for the same; and the Colts and Fillies, entered for the same, to be no more than four Years old the Grass before they run. Each Subscriber to pay his Stake on the Entrance Day of Richmond Races, or before starting, to the Stewards, or whom they shall appoint. [Signed] Cleveland, John Yorke, Warkworth, Wm. Fenwick, Darlington, P. Wentworth, Sim. Scroope, L. Dundas.*

Several of these names, of local aristocrats and worthies, occur in 'The Richmond Diary'.

Plays & Players

The 1760s was a time of particular popularity for the theatre, especially in London. The 'superstar' actor David Garrick was then at the height of his fame and influence, and he was portrayed by the artist Johann Zoffany, who also painted the king and queen and their older children in the mid-1760s. By the 1760s some English towns already had their own custom-built theatres, and although Richmond had to wait until 1788 for its own purpose-built playhouse – still surviving and famously known as The Georgian Theatre Royal – the town already boasted a flourishing theatrical culture by 1765.

The Diarist's entries, in her habitual detail, document this between 27 May and 15 July 1765. These identify the theatrical performances that she attended during this Richmond season. In this way she provides the most thorough account of the activities of the Yorkshire – and the provincial – theatre in this period.

'The Richmond Diary' indicates that in Richmond, at least two different groups of players were involved. Each of these has its distinctive repertoire, probably staged in different locations, with each being particularly conscious of how to attract substantial audiences during this early summer season.

The first players to arrive, by the last weekend in May, were a small travelling troupe, who present three very popular plays, two comedies – Farquar's *The Constant Couple* (first performed 1699) and Cibber's ballad opera *Damon and Phillida* (1729). The requisite Shakespeare offering was in this case *Richard III*, but now in its Georgian adaptation by Colley Cibber (1700).

The Diarist does not say where these performances took place but, since she has been offered tickets, lower and upper seating areas must have been available, and in the latter would have sat the Diarist and her friends. Any large room could have afforded this facility – the 'long room' of an inn (at a later date this could well have been the Bishop Blaize inn in the market place), the Toll Booth or the town hall.

Equally uncertain is the identity of this company of players. Such a travelling troupe might have played previously in Richmond, or even been 'regulars'. A possible candidate might be Tryphosa Wright's company that later, under Samuel Butler's management, performed regularly at the town's theatre. In the north Yorkshire of the 1760s, however, there were many such irregular troupes seeking one- or two-night stands.

It would seem that, performing in Richmond between 21 June and 15 July, was a second company of players, managed by Horatio Thomas McGeorge, a fairly well recognised, if not particularly outstanding, London actor and musician. These 'comedians' embodied a new sort of travelling professionalism. Although an ad hoc troupe, they were regular London actors, now touring the provinces during London's May to September recess. Probably many of them, as was certainly the case with McGeorge himself, had been recently performing there in the plays they now brought to Richmond.

Indeed, as their Richmond audience would have recognised, these plays had, and did, delight playgoers at London's Drury Lane and Covent Garden. Steele's *The Conscious Lovers* (first performed

1722) served as a model for the new sentimental comedy, and Henry Fielding's *The Miser* (1733) was so popular that, in its published form, was still being reprinted in the 1760s.

Even more revealing are the company's choice of farces. Both Samuel Foote's *The Mayor of Garrett* (1763) and Arthur Murphy's *The Citizen* (1761) were the works, only recently premiered in London, of two new, if contentious, dramatists. Understandably for his 'benefit' McGeorge chose one of the most successful of the period's warhorses, which drew in audiences wherever it was played, Thomas Otway's *Venice Preserved* (1682), a melodramatic romance, both politically dangerous and sexually conscious.

Again the Diarist does not say where she saw these productions but since, on the evening of Tuesday 25 June, she was in the town hall to hear McGeorge's rendition – he was one of its regular interpreters – of the *Lecture on Heads*, it is plausible that all this company's performances were given there. This would have been an astute move on McGeorge's part. Under the 1737 Licensing Act, plays were banned outside of the London patent theatres, unless mayors or justices could be persuaded to endorse their – and the actors' – suitability. In practise, actors provided grounds for such permission by performing what were labelled 'musical concerts' and 'lectures', with plays sandwiched between, for which there was no charge.

But the *Lecture on Heads* was no ordinary dramatic entertainment. It was a two-hour monologue which satirised, with illustrative papier maché heads, the law, the church and government, as embodied in their living representatives, in a feast of literary references. First performed in London in February 1764, the lecture took the city, and selected towns in England and America, by storm. Just over a year later it was presented, for one of the first times in the north of England, in Richmond town hall. What a compliment to that audience's breadth of outlook and their cultural standing. Among them sat the Diarist – despite the probable entrance ticket of 2s 6d.

If further evidence was needed of how Richmond's dramatic 'season' was avant-garde, it is to be found in the first appearance of McGeorge and his company in their 'play' at the Newbiggin house of Mrs Catherine Strickland. The actors would have performed songs and dramatic extracts to those who visited here. Such receptions were not unusual. By the 1760s the gentry and their wives were important supporters of the players, both at their stage performances and socially, which shows just how far rigid class-barriers were being crossed, through a growing recognition of new cultural values as expressed in theatrical presentations.

The Diarist's entries concerning plays and players are remarkable, underlining just how valued and welcomed such occasions were in the Richmond of the mid-1760s and, through her own knowledge and enthusiasm, how committed to them the Diarist was. Given her references to the friends that accompanied her to plays, she was far from unique.

The Military

The Richmond area has had important military associations since the Iron Age, with the huge Stanwick fortifications not far away, then throughout the Roman occupation with the unusually complex history of the fort Cataractonium, near Catterick, to the present and indeed the future, with Catterick Garrison being the largest military base in Europe and expected to expand further. A recent piece of national history occurred on 2 May 2015; Her Majesty Queen Elizabeth II was in Richmond Castle attending a private meeting as colonel-in-chief of seventy years standing with the Royal Lancers, recently amalgamated from two regiments, when she was informed of the birth that morning of her great-granddaughter Princess Charlotte.

Richmond in the 1760s also saw military activities, and the Diarist refers to soldiers in three categories. Of most interest to her are the young officers attending the musters of the North York Militia held regularly in Richmond. These were the mainstay of the assemblies and balls which took place to coincide with their presence. The second group are the regular soldiers attached to the militia based at its depot in Richmond. The third are troops passing through the town.

The impending presence of the first group is eagerly noticed. In both September 1764 and October 1765 we are informed that the militia are coming in to be exercised for a month. Sadly, the Emerson cousins, who come and stay with the Diarist at these times, appear to have more success in attracting officers' attention than she does. No fewer than four captains are either mentioned or indicated anonymously as dancing with, or attending on, the various Misses Emerson. When the Diarist attends the ball at the invitation of the officers on Thursday, 18 October, her dancing partner is a local man. Bell Emerson seems keen to go and watch the men training; the Diarist accompanies her on two of the three occasions this activity is mentioned.

The resident militiamen and their families were part of Richmond's social scene and their news was picked up over the teacups and recorded in 'The Richmond Diary'. 'Serjeant' John Dowson of the Richmondshire battalion was buried in September 1764, and in December 1765 Gerada, daughter of 'Serjeant' Alexander Campbell of the North Riding Militia succumbed to smallpox. Captain Moor and his family were visitors who came for tea with the Diarist.

The Diarist also implicitly has a link with the Durham Militia, not only through her connections with Teesdale, but also several of her acquaintances in Richmond and Easby are married to its soldiers.

In February 1765 three companies of foot soldiers, probably about 190 men in all, arrived in Richmond breaking their march south from Scotland to London. Possibly recently recruited from that traditional source of troops north of the border, it is likely that they marched down Frenchgate on their way into Richmond, and thus passed very close to the Diarist's lodgings.

Each company arrived one day, stayed overnight, and marched off the next morning, the next company arriving that day and so on, so as to make it possible for the inns in Richmond and the other towns on the route to billet them; troops then had no regular bases and had to be kept on the move. Since the ending of the Seven Years War in 1763, regiments had regularly been ordered to move around the country to let people know troops were available if required. Doubtless Richmond was used to seeing such a visible military presence at a period when there were protests, even riots, in other English towns.

Gardening

The Diarist clearly had a garden which she tended, but whether it was her own, or possibly Mr Morgotroy's market garden tended in exchange for produce, is unclear. Whichever, she spent time in it regularly, always noting how long she was on the task, from half an hour, an hour, and sensibly, never more than two hours.

There is only one reference to flowers – flower seeds arrived from Winston in May 1765 and were set immediately. All other entries relate either to soft fruit or are unspecified. She did some gardening in winter, presumably of the general tidying work that has to be done. There is one reference to weeding, in the rampant month of July 1765.

There must have been currant bushes already established in the garden as these were picked and shared with Mrs Panton in July 1764, and used by the Diarist for jelly in the August. The type of currants is not mentioned, but the jelly may suggest they were red.

July 1765 was clearly an excellent season for strawberries, which were picked ('pulled') from 3–20 July, in sufficient quantities to share with friends. The Wilsons had some for supper with the Diarist, as did some of their young ladies, but strawberries were also given to friends including Matty Beauly, who sent a theatre ticket as a thank you. There is no mention of strawberries when the journal begins on 24 July 1764, so either they had finished by then, or were only established later that year. Gooseberries cropped (seemingly for the first time) in August 1765 – they even made the Diarist ill!

It would seem that the Diarist's garden did not include tree fruits, for baskets of apples and pears were sent over from the orchard at Winston rectory on three occasions in the autumn of 1765, the last batch being apples for Christmas on 23 December. The only vegetables mentioned are the 'pease' which were 'scalded' at Mrs Mawer's in August 1764.

The Diarist's keen interest in gardening is reflected in her starting her daily entries with a note of the weather. She particularly records frost and snow, especially if experienced at unusual times of the year, such as in late September and late October 1764, as well as during the winter months when such would be expected. Violent storms also feature, including some which brought the hail that gardeners so dislike for the damage it causes.

Illnesses & Medical Treatments

'The Richmond Diary' contains many entries recording ill health, of the writer and her Mama – her sister seems to enjoy good health, suffering only a cold in the course of the diary. Mama was in generally good health for an older lady, though she had a painful back, attacks of giddiness in the head and the 'gravel' in her urinary tract. She also tended to get heavy colds, which made her 'badly', a present of a bottle of syrup of cloves may have been intended to help this.

Mama seems to have been indulged with a fire burning in her room much of the time, and if the Diarist is unwell she goes to sit in Mama's room. Mama's doctor was Christopher Wayne, the son of a Stokesley medical man who had settled in Richmond and become a member of the town's establishment, serving as mayor in 1771. He was married to Jane Metcalfe, a member of an old and wealthy Richmond family of apothecaries. They had no children but he continued the family medical dynasty by taking a number of apprentices.

Christopher Wayne is always respectfully called Mr Wayne in the diary. He is noted as 'bleeding' Mama in July 1765, after she had had a cold for about ten days. In April 1765 a letter was received from cousin Bell, with a 'melancholy account' of the health of her father, Revd John Emerson. The Diarist was asked to get some treatment for him from Dr Wayne, presumably considered superior to any medical practitioner in Barnard Castle, the nearest town to Winston. The medicine was an 'electuary' or paste sweetened with honey containing some unappetising drug. It seems to have had the desired effect, for Revd Emerson lived on until 1774. The Diarist knew the Waynes socially, for she and her cousin Bell had, in October 1764, drunk tea at Mrs Wayne's.

The Diarist was frequently unwell, although she seems not to have had any chronic illnesses, as her health recovered each time. The heavy colds could have been partly caused by the house being damp and chilly in the areas not heated as often as Mama's room, and the pains in her head and face could indicate sinusitis. The 'balm of Gilead' given to her would provide a soothing aromatic concoction. There is no reference to a cough accompanying these respiratory infections, so it is unlikely that tuberculosis was involved.

On several occasions she was in bed for a few days, and in August 1765 had a week being very poorly, getting up only to have her bed made, having no sleep some nights, and sending for the doctor, who visited three days running. The Diarist's doctor was James Pringle, the medical practitioner to the Roman Catholic residents and a well-qualified 'doctor of physic'. He was also a friend, and paid social calls; his marriage to Rosa, daughter of Richmond apothecary John Nandike, is noted in January 1765. He had recently built a handsome new Georgian townhouse on the north side of Newbiggin.

Illnesses of other people are occasionally mentioned. The Diarist's great friend Mrs Mawer's unspecified health scare early in August 1764 caused great concern, and poor Matty Beauly's jaundice sounds very nasty. Mr Wilson suffered from rheumatism. Children of the town dying during an outbreak of smallpox warranted several diary entries.

Smallpox, the major killer disease of the Georgian period, was no respecter of social class. Caused largely by contact with the sores which developed, often through contaminated bedding or clothing, one might expect it mainly to have affected the poor, but as it could be spread via respiratory droplets, the gentry were also frequent victims. About one third of cases resulted in death.

Some survivors suffered blindness or deafness, but almost all were significantly disfigured by pockmarks on their skins, often on the face. At the end of the eighteenth century, Edward Jenner famously developed a vaccine which, subsequently, would make smallpox the only disease eradicated worldwide by this means.

Church Services

The Diarist demonstrates a close attachment to St Mary's parish church, situated off Frenchgate. In the eighteenth century the building had the same 'footprint' as today, although its roofs were much lower before the Victorian restoration. The interior was very different however, no orderly rows of open pews as now, but a jumble of privately owned galleries and box pews all of different dates. Many of the better houses in Richmond had their own pew in the church, and ownership of it was transferred with the deeds of a house. A contentious issue was where the not-so-privileged parishioners could sit. Judging by the number of times the Diarist attends church, it has to be assumed that she – and her guests – had an entitlement to sit in a specific location, though it is not known if Bowes Hall had its own private pew.

The Georgian pattern of church services was also different from today, centred around the prayer book services of Morning Prayer and Evening Prayer, with the emphasis on the sermon or a homily. Holy Communion was only celebrated about four times a year – at major festivals such as Christmas, Easter and Whitsuntide, plus perhaps Harvest or Michaelmas.

The Diarist attends church on Sundays unless she is ill or the weather is extremely bad, more often than not going to both services. When Bell Emerson stayed with her for the month of October 1765 the two attended church together, but Mama joins the Diarist at church on a Sunday only infrequently. Sometimes the Diarist also went to church on a Friday, when Morning Prayer included a litany, and Mama often went with her to this, and once Mama and the Diarist went on a Tuesday.

Church festivals are only occasionally mentioned, such as Ash Wednesday, Good Friday, Easter Sunday and Whit Sunday 1765. In June 1765 the Diarist made a special journey over to Winston to attend church there, presumably for some important but unspecified reason connected with Revd John Emerson, his health, or his family. Given her closeness to this uncle, and her Smith relations including several clergymen, it seems somewhat surprising that she never mentions who took the services.

For much of the second half of the eighteenth century the rector of Richmond was the distinguished, charismatic and somewhat controversial Revd Francis Blackburne. The Diarist only mentions him once, obliquely, when she visits the rectory seeking his daughter Jane. As Revd Blackburne was also Archdeacon of Cleveland and a Prebendary of York, he would frequently be away from Richmond and doubtless had various curates who would take services. His income from Richmond alone was not inconsiderable at £66 a year, plus rectorial tithes, so he was well able to afford to pay his assistants.

The Diarist dutifully attends church on Monday, 3 June 1765 for the Visitation, a formal inspection of parishes regularly carried out, either by the Bishop of Chester (in which diocese Richmond was at the time), or the long-serving Archdeacon of Richmond, Samuel Peploe, son of the previous Bishop of Chester. Visitation sermons were often published, and this is the only service for which the Diarist records the preacher – 'Mr Peacock'. This is probably John Peacock, a curate of Revd John Emerson's at Stainton rectory who also served as the vicar of Hilton church, both of which were within Francis Blackburne's Archdeaconry of Cleveland. It would seem that Blackburne, a highly regarded preacher, gave the young man the opportunity to make his mark. Another of Revd Emerson's curates, Revd Thomas Holmes Tidy, is obliquely mentioned in the journal.

The only Richmond clergyman explicitly mentioned in 'The Richmond Diary' is Revd John Stoupe, the first perpetual curate appointed to Trinity chapel in the market place after it had been repaired and brought back into use in 1755. This restoration had been at the instigation of Francis Blackburne, who preached there on Wednesdays in winter. Stoupe seems to have been a middle-aged man in the 1760s, and was probably single. He paid for several children 'on the parish' to attend a local school. Stoupe is mentioned only as a courier who, in December 1765, took a letter from the Diarist's sister to Nanny Smith, probably in London. Perhaps Stoupe was going 'home' to relatives for Christmas. Her friend Revd Christopher Nichols was based in Cambridge.

Births, Marriages and Deaths

'The Richmond Diary' contains numerous references to these major events in the lives of the Diarist's contemporaries. She notes the arrival of babies to several of her friends, including the daughter of mercer Thomas Simpson, the son of her close friends the Newsams, and she visited Hannah Cowling who was 'lying in' after producing her sixteenth child, baby Moses. There are no references to baptisms in the diary, although the church records of such have been extensively used to flesh out the bones of the Diarist's entries.

Small children often visited the Diarist with their parents, George Hutchinson's little boy and Betty Taylor's little girl are mentioned several times, and the newly-acquired skills of children attending the dancing school are dutifully noted. Childhood mortality is inevitably present in the background to the diary, particularly when there is an outbreak of smallpox, and even the heiress to the Yorke family sadly failed to survive.

'The Richmond Diary' contains important information, often implicit rather than explicit, about how our Georgian ancestors regarded weddings. The Diarist seems not to have attended any weddings in the period covered by the diary, but those of two people important to her do occur. The first is on Tuesday, 8 January 1765, when her good friend, the Roman Catholic doctor, James Pringle, got married to Rosa Nandike, the daughter of his colleague, the apothecary John Nandike. The Diarist notes it, but makes no comment about attending. It could be argued that there were two factors influencing the couple having a quiet wedding, one that he was a Roman Catholic, although the ceremony had to take place in the parish church, and second that he was marrying for the second time, as a widower. However, we are later told that it was already the custom to call the bride's attendant a bridesmaid.

Six months later, however, a wedding took place which it would seem the Diarist was hoping to attend, or at least it appears so as she had just bought a new hat! This was the marriage, on 11 June 1765, of her beloved cousin Jenny Emerson, who married Thomas Emerson Headlam of Gateshead in Winston Church, where Jenny's father was rector. The ceremony was performed by his curate, Thomas Holmes Tidy, presumably so Rev Emerson could give his daughter away. That wedding cakes were then the norm, at least for quite prosperous families, is shown by the Diarist receiving a piece of wedding cake via Jenny's sister, Fanny, a few days later.

The Diarist gives us far more information on deaths. She mentions, directly or indirectly, almost all of the burials which took place during the period the diary covers, around fifty of them. It is tempting to wonder if the writer was obsessed by deaths, but the answer is probably not. Her links with the clergy meant that she was very aware of how much their role then, as nowadays, was concerned with conducting funeral services, and as her accommodation was in the Frenchgate area, she was bound often to see funeral processions heading sadly towards the parish church.

Richmond churchyard then received almost all burials of those who died in the town, whether or not they were permanently based there. In the era before railways, few people could afford to transport a body to a different place of burial, and only the Quakers had their own burial ground in the town. The frequency of burials and the practise of usually burying people within a couple of days of death, meant that interments took place at all sorts of times, and not only on weekdays but also on Sundays and even on Christmas Day 1765.

Many of the deaths mentioned by the Diarist seem to be of people with whom she had some connection, either a family she knew personally – or knew of, such as a shoemaker or tailor – or the person's death had been a topic of conversation, such as when children were dying of smallpox. The fact that her spellings of their names often differs slightly from those in the parish register suggests that she was writing a phonetic version of a name she had heard discussed orally. It seems that when she uses the term 'funeral', it means she attended the service, and when she refers to someone being 'buried' it means she knows it happens without having been there herself.

Roman Catholics were buried in the churchyard alongside their Protestant neighbours, and the entry for Tuesday, 18 September 1764 includes: 'At 2 o'clock I went to Mrs Sandbridge's funeral. Dr Pringle came home with me and drank tea'. The parish register records the burial of 'Mrs Sandbirch widow a papist'. The Diarist's friend Dr Pringle was himself a Roman Catholic and particularly provided medical support to the town's Catholic residents. It is likely that this was one of the genteel widows for whom Richmond was such a popular retirement location, and as she may not have known many people, the good Dr Pringle possibly sought the Diarist's support at Mrs Sandbirch's funeral and burial, which presumably were conducted by a Roman Catholic priest.

We know that Dr Pringle sought her support for another lady who would seem not to have had family able to attend her obsequies. The entry for Monday, 12 August 1765 includes: 'Dr Pringle's servant came to invite me to Miss Hall's funeral to be a bearer: we had white hoods, scarfes and gloves'. The parish register entry reads: 'Miss Hall of Edinburgh', so the lady was indeed far from home. The white attire for a pallbearer is typical of a spinster's funeral at the period. The term does not relate to someone helping to carry the coffin, as now, but for those who escorted it to hold the pall, or cloth, used in the past to cover a coffin, to stop it trailing on the ground.

An interesting reference to a death concerns the Yorke family of The Green. Under Saturday, 4 May 1765 the Diarist somewhat blandly notes: 'Miss York dead', and then comments on Friday, 10 May: 'Miss York buried in a very private manner. 10 o'clock at night.' This was Sophia Anne, daughter of John Yorke and his wife Sophia Glynne of Wales, who had married in 1763. John and Sophia were only to have this one child, who died at 16 months. She was buried in the family vault in the parish church, and her coffin and delicate lace bonnet were seen when the vault was rediscovered in 1988.

An unusual case of someone being taken for burial elsewhere occurred on 16 September 1765, and it is not the actual funeral that the Diarist recorded: 'At 11 o'clock a hearse and two post-chaises went past with Miss Pinkney to Darlington whear [sic] she is to be buried.' Mary Pinckney was buried at St Cuthbert's church in Darlington that day.

The Manuscript

The manuscript was purchased from a dealer in 1988 by the historian L. P. Wenham, who carefully transcribed and indexed it. He did quite a lot of research on its contents but had not overcome the many dilemmas it poses before his death early in 1990. His transcription remains the basis of this work with a few amendments in the light of further study.

The manuscript consists of fifty-six pages, all closely covered with the same neat ink handwriting. The pages are 6½in x 8in, cut down from larger sheets. The handmade, and laid, linen rag paper is of good quality, and was carefully lined in pencil by the author, who sewed it together as a slim book. Each page also has a ruled left hand margin in which the dates are written. Given that the manuscript has few erasures or ink smudges, it would seem most likely that the final text derived from original notes or preliminary jottings or drafts.

At a later date the manuscript was placed in card boards which were covered in blue linen, crudely-sewn and labelled in a much inferior manner, presumably by an owner to whom it passed by descent.

'The Richmond Diary' with Commentary

The text is, as far as possible, a literal transcription of the original. This means that certain words will appear in variant spellings, e.g. 'recd' (received), pul[l]ing, sup[p]er. In the eighteenth century, dictionary-agreed spelling had not been finalised, hence 'strawberrys'. Where the Diarist's usage is confusing or difficult for the reader to follow, [sic] is inserted or a letter [l] to modernise the spelling. The diary provides invaluable period evidence of punctuation and word usage, e.g. 'thust' for 'is just' (come home etc.)

For the reader's convenience the days and dates of the entries in the diary have been italicised. The authors' commentary, margined to the right, is interspersed with the diary text.

Tuesday July 24 1764 The Journal Continued.

In the Garden an hour, receiv'd a letter from Miss Jenny Emerson, return'd an answer. Miss Milbank came home with Miss Mawer and stay'd the day rain in the Eve. Christopher Wadkens wife buried. Mrs and Miss Mawer came in for half an hour.

24 July 1764

The opening entry of what survives of 'The Richmond Diary' sets the scene for the pattern that follows. Time spent in the garden is noted. A letter is received from one of the Diarist's Emerson cousins in Winston, and a reply despatched immediately. The names of those whose social company she shared are recorded. As often there is a comment on one of the burials which frequently took place in St Mary's churchyard. Christopher Watkins was a tailor whose workshop the Diarist probably knew, he would remarry in May 1766.

Wednesday 25 very dull day, Mrs Panton, Mrs and Miss Mawer drank tea with us. A Girl of Nelson's buried.

Mrs Panton was particularly friendly with the Diarist's closest friends, Mrs Mawer and her daughter Bridget. The next burial was of John Nelson's daughter Alice.

Thursday 26 rain great part of the day, after dinner Mrs Mawer and Miss came in, I drank Tea there with Mrs Panton, Mrs Chapman and Mrs Sewdale.

Friday 27 in the Garden, a Shower of rain, sent Mrs Panton a plate of Currants. I set an hour at Mrs Mawer's to se Mr Pickerin the Painter, take Miss Mawer's Picture. In the Eve Mrs Panton came in, after Supper Miss Mawer set an hour with us.

27 July 1764

Mrs Panton receives some of the currants from the garden. Mrs and Miss Mawer are presented to us as an affluent economic group by this record. Henry Pickering was a well-known portrait painter working in northern circles, and one of some quality, having been tutored by Thomas Hudson, a pupil of Reynolds, and in all probability having been on a Grand Tour. He employed skilled drapery painters to assist him with his sitters' clothes. His sitters were considered mainly to be squires, baronets and aldermen, so 'The Richmond Diary' extends the range of his known commissions. Pictures signed and dated by him are mainly 1740–70, so his portraits of the Mawers fall towards the end of his working life. York Art Gallery (York Museums Trust) has portraits by him of Alderman James Rowe and his wife, both dated 1752; Rowe was Lord Mayor of York in 1749 and 1768.

Saturday 28 Miss Mawer and I down Street at Mr Newsham's to se the tumbler, came home in a Shower of Rain, my Sister got a letter from Miss Emerson & one from Miss Fanny. I went in to Mrs Mawer's in the Eve.

28 July 1764

James Newsam, a grocer, was a friend of the Diarist's. Outside his shop on the High Row of the market place would be a prominent location for a street entertainer to perform on Richmond's market day. More of the Diarist's family are now introduced to us – her sister, and two more cousins, the eldest Emerson sister Elizabeth and the youngest Frances.

Sunday 29 fine day, at Church Morn & Eve, after dinner Miss Mawer came in. I maid a visit to Mrs Bowes.

29 July 1764

Sally Bowes, the daughter of the Diarist's landlady, Mrs Readhead, had recently given birth to her second daughter, Sarah, now 16 weeks old.

July 1764 Monday 30 fine day. In the garden, two hours, after dinner Mrs Mawer and Miss came in.

30 July 1764

The fine weather encouraged the Diarist to spend two hours in the garden. It is significant that gardening is the only activity for which she records the time spent, which may suggest this is a commercial rather than a leisure occupation.

Tuesday 31 Rain great part of day. Mama and I drank tea at Mrs Mawer's.

August 1 Rain all the Morn. I drank tea at Mrs Mawer's, thither Mrs Readhead and the Painter.

1 August 1764

Mrs Mawer's portrait painter is attracting a lot of interest among the tea-drinking group. Mrs Readhead is probably the Mawers' landlady too.

Thursday 2 Cold rain, in the garden an hour, after dinner Miss Mawer came to ask me to go in, Mrs Mawer is not well, Mr Key Mawer sent Mama a Moor Cock. He drank tea with us, at Mrs Mawer's; in the Morn Mrs Colingwood gave us a call.

2 August 1764

The Diarist is sufficiently close to Mrs Mawer to be called in by her daughter when the older lady is unwell, and when her son Kay is visiting. Mama's treat of a moorcock (a male red grouse), is a bird only found on the heather moorlands of northern Britain.

Friday 3 in the Garden, a very Cold Shower of rain, I drank Tea with Mrs Wilson and Miss Nendike, Mrs Blakeborough there. Mama, Sister and I invited to Mrs Mawer's to a Scalding of pease.

3 August 1764

Today's entry introduces us for the first time to Mrs Wilson whose school for young ladies will soon form a major part of the Diarist's life. Rosa, daughter of Richmond apothecary John Nandike, would, next January, become the second wife of the Diarist's doctor and friend James Pringle, whose first wife had died in 1759. Mrs Blegborough, formerly Grace Hutchinson of Hill House in Richmond, was the wife of another Richmond medical man, Henry Blegborough. Mrs Mawer seems to have recovered sufficiently to host the traditional sociable feast of 'peascalding', which consisted of extracting, with the teeth, peas from boiled young pods, dipped in melted butter and salt.

Saturday 4 down Street at Miss Dixon's, stay'd to se the mountebank, after dinner Miss Mawer came in. E Beautyment drank Tea with us. I spent the Even at Mrs Mawer's, rainey night.

4 August 1764

Another close friend of the Diarist's was Miss Faith Dixon, a draper. Her premises, consisting of a shop with a separate house behind it, was in the market place. Another street entertainer, this time selling possibly somewhat dubious patent medicines, had been drawn to Richmond on its market day. Young Elspith Beautyment may have been full of her forthcoming marriage.

Sunday 5 dull day. At Church Morn and Even. Miss Mawer came in after dinner, in the Even Miss Mawer cald upon me to walk in Mr York's Gardens, we thust got home before the rain came on.

5 August 1764

The Diarist visited the famous landscaped gardens of the Yorke family on the Green in Richmond, which were open to the Georgian public on certain summer Sundays, with Bridget Mawer who seems to have known the Yorke family socially.

Monday 6 Shower of rain in the Morn. I drank Tea at Mrs Pantons, in the Even went into Mrs Mawer's.

August 7 in the Garden two hours. I got a letter from C. F. Emerson, down Street at Miss Dixon's to get some ribband to send to Winston. I drank Tea at Mrs M.

7 August 1764

> *The letter from the Diarist's cousin Fanny Emerson presumably asked for the urgent despatch to Winston of ribbons – the Diarist's friend Faith Dixon clearly stocked better ribbons than were available in Teesdale.*

Wednesday 8 in the Garden two hours, in the Eve Mrs Panton set half an hour, after Supper Miss Mawer came in.

Thursday 9 in the garden puling currants for jelly, after dinner Mrs Bosamworth call'd. Shower of rain in the Eve, Mrs Mawer came in. Mrs Jane Geldard buried.

9 August 1764

> *The garden is producing quantities of currants, presumably red ones for jelly. Jane Geldard was the licensee of the Griffin Inn, on the site of no. 6 Market Place. Her will shows that she made her own malt as well as brewing her own ale.*

Friday 10 dull day I walk'd down Street, cal'd at Matty's, drank Tea at Miss Dixon's, in the Eve Miss Mawer came to ask me to go in, she has got Mrs Storey to make her a new neglijey. Shower of rain.

10 August 1764

> *Matty Beauly, innkeeper of the King's Arms on the north side of the market place, was another close friend of the Diarist's. The 'neglijey' is a phonetic spelling of what was presumably boasted about over the teacups by the affluent Bridget Mawer. A 'neglejay', or loose informal gown worn by women in the eighteenth century, was not the dressing gown or 'negligee' in the modern sense. Mrs Storey is the only dressmaker named in 'The Richmond Diary'.*

Saturday 11 down Street at Miss Dixon's. Shower of rain, drank tea at Mrs Mawer's.

Sunday 12 at Church in the Morn, rain great part of the afternoon. Mrs Readhead came in, Matty Bauley came with George Hutchinson little boy, for half an hour. Mrs Wilson and Miss Nindike gave us a call, after supper Miss Mawer set an hour with us.

12 August 1764

Matty Beauly had a day off from inn-keeping on Sundays. It is unclear what her link was with George Hutchinson, an agent for Sir Lawrence Dundas of Aske Hall. The little boy, then aged 4, would attend Richmond Grammar School and go up to Trinity College, Cambridge, where he became a Fellow.

Monday 13 Violent rain, hail and Thunder. Mrs Mawer and Miss drank Tea with us.

Tuesday Aug 14 rain, hail and Thunder great part of the day. Mama had a letter from Nanny Smith, one inside for Mr F. Allen by young Mr Gail, from London. After Tea Miss Mawer came in. William Garthwhate buried.

14 August 1764

The reported correspondence brings us more family members. Nanny Smith, the Diarist's sister-in-law, was writing from London to Mama (her mother-in-law) and Francis Allen, her brother. 'Young Mr Gail' who brought the letters north to save postage is probably Henry Gale (1744–1821), son of Roger Gale of Scruton, who was married to Catherine Crowe of Kiplin, and grandson of Roger Gale the antiquarian. Young Henry would marry Mary Dalton of Hauxwell in 1779. William Garthwaite was a staymaker with premises in the Toll Booth, a large Georgian commercial building which stood in the market place.

Wednesday 15 down Street at Miss Dixon's & Wrathers. Call'd at Mr F. Allen's with Nanny Smith's letter, had words with Miss Strickland and Capn Urwen. In the Even Miss Mawer came in, we had a walk round the Castle, rainy night.

15 August 1764

It was a serious shopping day with visits to two drapers. Miss Strickland was one of several sisters living with their widowed mother in Newbiggin. They were a Roman Catholic family. The evening outing was round Castle Walk, an early Georgian promenade which afforded fine views of the Swale valley.

Thursday 16 rain great part of the day. Mrs Panton drank tea with us, in the Eve. Mrs Mawer and Miss came in.

Friday 17 rain all the morning, Mrs, Miss and Mr Kay Mawer drank Tea here, the two ladies set til 8 o'clock. I wrote to Cousin Fanny, sent a book.

17 August 1764

One of the few occasions when three members of the Mawer family visit, though Kay, a young clergyman of about thirty, seems not to have wanted to spend as many hours over the tea cups as his mother and sister. Richmond was fortunate enough to be served by a good bookshop, so the Diarist could easily obtain a book for her Winston relatives.

Saturday 18 rainy Morn. I recved a letter from Miss J. Emerson, I went into Mrs Mawers for half an hour. Betty Beautyment drank tea with us, my Sister wrote to Winston.

18 August 1764

Letters are flying back and forth to Winston, one from Jenny was replied to by the Diarist's sister, usually the scribe for the family. Betty Beautyment had probably brought butter to sell in the market that day, and afterwards had a well-earned social meeting with the Diarist and her mother.

Sunday 19 at Church Morn & Eve. Several Showers of rain, Mama and I drank Tea at Mrs Mawers, we receivd a letter from Matthew Graham. Miss Mawer and I had a walk in Mr York's Gardens, when we got home I was taken ill in the gr......s [sic]. Miss M came in after Supper.

19 August 1764

As well as attending church twice, the Diarist again enjoyed a walk with Bridget Mawer in the Yorke family's famous landscaped garden.

Monday 20 very ill all day, after dinner Mr Moor gave us a call in his way home from his brother's Funeral, after tea Mrs Mawer and Miss came in.

20 August 1764

Rev Matthew Moore, who held several incumbencies in Teesdale, including those of Rokeby and Barningham, was the younger brother of Revd James Moore, perpetual curate of Arkengarthdale north of Reeth, who had been buried there on 17 August 1764. Matthew would live on until 1792.

Tuesday 21 much better today. Nanny washing, very fine warm day, in the Eve Mrs Mawer came in, after Supper, Miss.

<u>21 August 1764</u>

The pleasant weather has made the Diarist feel better after her recent illness, and has encouraged the household maid Nanny to start washing, one of few specific mentions of her labours.

Wednesday Augt 22 fine warm day, Mama and I walk'd into the Paddock met with Mrs Mawer there, in the Morn Mrs Bosamworth cal'd. I got a letter from Cousin F. Emerson. After dinner Miss Mawer came to ask me to drink Tea.

<u>22 August 1764</u>

The Paddock was probably a field behind the parish church, as Mama seems not to have been able to walk far.

Thursday 23 Fine day, Mama and I in the Paddock, in the Eve Mrs Mawer and Miss came in.

Friday 24 Ironing all the Morn. Charming day. In the Eve Mrs Mawer and Miss.

<u>24 August 1764</u>

The washing of three days ago is now followed for two days (Friday and Saturday) by the inevitable task of ironing, which it would seem the Diarist undertook, or helped with, herself.

Saturday 25 Ironing in the Morn, I receivd a letter from Betty Robinson from Barnard Castle to inform me she would be at Richmond to stay with us the Races. I drank Tea with Miss Mawer in the Eve, down Street.

<u>25 August 1764</u>

Elizabeth Robinson was a young relative of Revd John Emerson of Winston. She was inviting herself to stay in Richmond for the races in September. The Diarist wrote back in the affirmative a few days later. The Diarist's Emerson cousins would also come to stay then.

Sunday 26 at Church Morn and Eve, a few drops of rain. The two Mrs Colinwoods drank Tea with us, in the Eve Miss Mawer call'd upon me to walk.

Monday 27 fine day down at the China Shop in the morning, drank Tea at Mrs Simpson's, along with Miss Mawer in the Eve Mrs Mawer came in and Matty Beauly.

27 August 1764

Most references to shops relate to drapers, but here there is one to a shop selling china – the social pastime of tea drinking required fashionable teacups.

Augt 28 in the Garden fine day. I wrote to Betty Robinson after dinner. Mrs Mawer and Miss came in to ask Mama and me to drink Tea, in the Eve I went down Street.

Wednesday 29 a shower of rain in the Morn, dull day. I recd a letter from Cousin Bell Emerson. Nanny busy cleaning the house for the Races. I drank Tea at Mrs Mawer's, after Tea they came in with me, and set til 8 o'clock.

29 August 1764

Preparations for the visitors coming to stay for the races generate another specific reference to the work of Nanny the maid. Every inch of space would be needed to accommodate all the visitors.

Thursday 30 tolerable day, Mama and I drank Tea at Mrs Mawer's. Mrs Readhead there, after Supper Miss Mawer came in.

30 August 1764

Mama must take the opportunity of taking tea with her friends before she takes herself away from Richmond for the duration of the races.

Friday 31 fine day, I recd a letter from Miss Bell Emerson by there maid who came to Town with Moorgame to Matty's. After tea Miss Mawer came in to ask me to go down Street.

31 August 1764

Expensive postage has been saved by the Emerson family's maid when she came into Richmond. The letter was doubtless finalising arrangements for the Teesdale contingent coming to stay for the races. The Emersons were, like the Diarist, generous in supplying Matty Beauly with luxuries, such as grouse, for the meals she provided at her inn, which would soon be extra busy with people arriving for the races. The phrase 'down Street' had come into popular usage by this period, and is used repeatedly in the diary. It clearly meant going into the market place, usually to do some window-shopping. Here the fashion-conscious Bridget Mawer was keen to see the new stocks of goods the Richmond drapers would have got in for the influx of prosperous visitors to the imminent races.

Sept 1 fine day. After Tea Mrs Panton gave us a call. Mrs Mawer and Miss came in, Mrs Mawer goes out of Town tomorrow til after the Races. I recd a letter from A. Nichols.

1 September 1764

Mrs Mawer, like Mama, prefers to avoid the excitement of the Richmond races. The Diarist's friend Alice Nichols lived in London.

Sunday 2 at Church in the Morn, after dinner Miss Mawer came in before Tea. Miss Bell Emerson, Miss Fanny Emerson and Miss Robinson arrivd to stay the Races Week with us. After Supper Miss Mawer came in, in the Eve Dr. Pringle.

2 September 1764

The house is filling up with three guests from Teesdale. The sociable Roman Catholic doctor, James Pringle, not yet remarried, evidently enjoyed the company of five young women.

Monday 3 dull day, my Cousins and I down Street, Miss Mawer drank Tea with us, we had a walk to Easby. Mrs Panton call'd upon Miss Emersons.

3 September 1764

The Emerson girls are always keen to inspect the shops 'down Street'. The five young women also use part of the day before the start of the races to walk to Easby, where they would almost certainly meet people they knew. Mrs Panton knows the Diarist has houseguests for the races.

Septr 4 Miss Bell Emerson, Miss Fanny Emerson, Miss Robinson and I down Street cald upon Mrs Simpson. Miss Fanny Emerson upon the Moor in Mr Witham's Coach. The 50*L* won by Mr Alcock's roan mare *Blackbird*. Miss Emersons and I at the Assembly, all danc'd. Miss Bell Emerson, and Mr Hill, Miss Fanny and Mr Robinson, Mr Anderson and Me, we came home a little after 12 o'Clock.

4 September 1764

More shopping or window-shopping in the morning, before the races in the afternoon. The Diarist shares the excitement of the youngest, and most boisterous, of the Emerson girls, enjoying the treat of a ride up to the racecourse in a coach. The winning horse of that day's most valuable race is noted, also the pairings at the following assembly, and the late hour this finished.

Wednesday 5 Mr Hill and Mr Robinson at Breakfast. We made a Morning Visit to Mrs Newsham, and cal'd upon Miss Cornforth, when we came home Miss Fanny Emerson was come. After dinner Miss Bell went home. The 50*L* was won by Mr Hutton's bay colt *Whitworth*. Miss Jenny, Miss Fanny and my self at the Assembly all danc'd Captain Norton and Miss Jenny Emerson, Mr Hill Miss Fanny, Mr Thornborough and my Self.

5 September 1764

Two of the group's male partners, Mr Hill and Mr Robinson, probably distant relations of the Emersons, are entertained to breakfast, presumably being sufficiently intimate to stay somewhere in the same complex of accommodation. Another Emerson cousin, Jenny, has arrived to replace Bell. Again the horses and dancing partners are recorded.

Thursday 6 Mr Thornborough and Mr Hill at Breakfast. Miss Witham cal'd upon Miss Emersons, Mr Buckton gave us a call, and Mr Carr. The Gold Cup was won by Mr Hutton's *Silvio*. The same day the Sweepstakes was won by Mr Wentworth Bay Colt. All at the Assembly, all danc'd. Miss Jenny Emerson Mr Robinson, Miss Fanny Mr Hill, Mr Thornborough and my Self. A very Genteel Meeting, and remarkable fine weather.

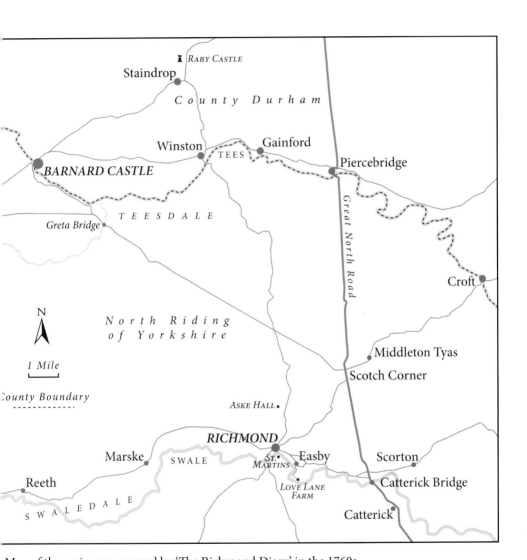

Map of the main area covered by 'The Richmond Diary' in the 1760s

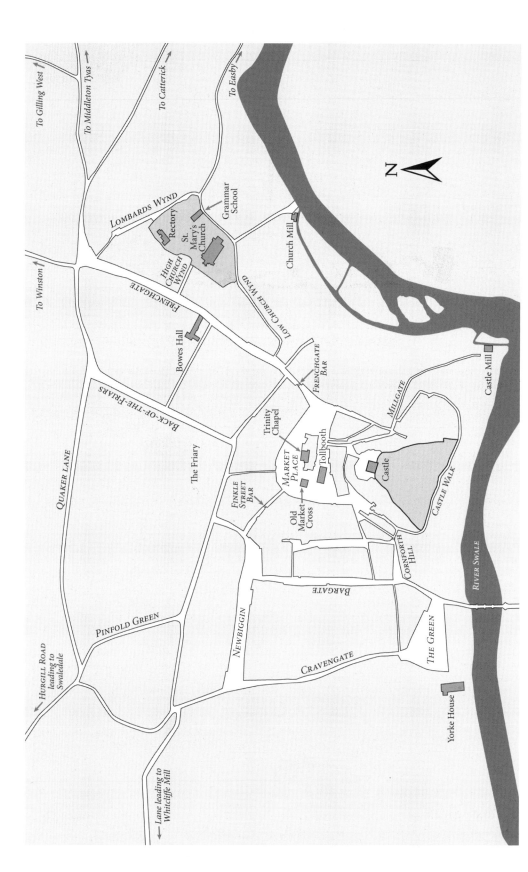

Map of Richmond in 2016

The opening page of 'The Richmond Diary'

Winston Bridge of 1762–3, crossing the river Tees. Based on a contemporary painting

A surviving Richmond
Georgian Shop Front

A London Draper's Shop trade card (Granger Historical Picture Archive/Alamy)

Thomas Bewick woodcut of the finishing post of a horse race, of a type used on race cards for various Georgian racecourses (a private collection)

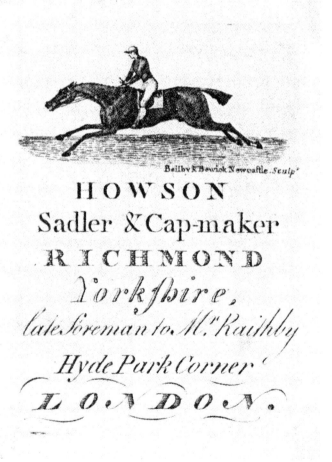

Thomas Bewick woodcut of a Richmond saddler's trade card (Thomas Bewick Birthplace Trust in association with St Paul's Bibliographies, Winchester Omnigraphics Inc. Detroit, 1981)

Thomas Bewick woodcut of a capercaillie, a large type of grouse, similar to the moorco mentioned in the diary (Thom Bewick Birthplace Trust in association with St Paul's Bibliographies, Winchester Omnigraphics Inc. Detroit, 19

Stage-coach notice, 1731

BIRMINGHAM
STAGE-COACH,

In Two Days and a half; begins May the 24th, 1731.

SET out from the *Swan-Inn* in *Birmingham*, every *Monday* at six a Clock in the Morning, through *Warwick, Banbury* and *Alesbury*, to the *Red Lion Inn* in *Aldersgate street, London,* every *Wednesday* Morning: And returns from the said *Red Lion Inn* every *Thursday* Morning at five a Clock the same Way to the *Swan-Inn* in *Birmingham* every *Saturday*, at 21 Shillings each Passenger, and 18 Shillings from *Warwick,* who has liberty to carry 14 Pounds in Weight, and all above to *pay One Penny a Pound.*
        Perform'd (if God permit)

By Nicholas Rothwell.

James Gillray cartoon of Militia Soldiers 1796 (Reproduced courtesy of the North Yorkshire County Record Office)

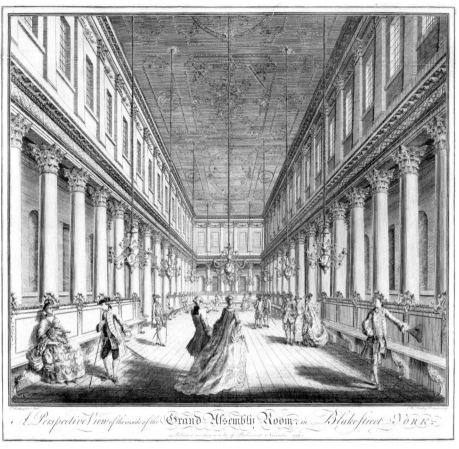

William Lindley's engraving of the interior of the York Assembly Rooms, 1759 (York Museums Trust)

Yorke House, the mansion of the Yorke family on The Green

St Mary's Parish Church, Richmon in Georgian time

Again two of the male guests share breakfast. There are yet more visitors to the house party. The Gold Cup was the most valuable prize of the Richmond Races, and this year was won by a famous horse bred by John Hutton, the squire of Marske in Swaledale. 'Silvio', who had won many great races, had come second in the Gold Cup for the four previous years, but at last triumphed. That evening's assembly would be quite an event – hence the remark 'A very Genteel Meeting'.

Friday 7 Mr Hill at breakfast, Miss Jenny Cornforth cal'd upon us, we walk down with her to Mrs Bowes to se the Cup, it is a very handsome one. After dinner Miss Mawer came in, and set an hour, Miss Emersons, Miss Robinson and I had a walk. Miss Mawer came in after Supper. Mama got a letter from John Parry.

Jane, or Jenny, was the sister of William Cornforth whose horse would win a race the following year, hence her interest in Richmond's most important racing trophy, the Gold Cup, displayed in the town for all the visitors to see. The Cornforths were a Teesdale family; three sisters: Dorothy, Ann and Jane would all remain single. Jane, who settled in Gainford, was probably staying for the race week with her brother Thomas who had moved into Richmond to carry out legal work for Sir Lawrence Dundas of Aske Hall. Now the races are over, Mama can return to Richmond.

Sept 8 I went in to se Mrs Mawer she is thust got home. After dinner down Street at the Shops. Miss Emersons, Miss Robinson and I drank Tea at Mrs Mawer's.

Not only has Mama returned as the races finish, but Mrs Mawer is back too. However the Teesdale houseguests are still here.

Sunday 9 Miss Emersons, Miss Robinson and I at Church Morn and Eve. After Tea Miss Emersons went home, Miss Robinson and I had a walk, Miss Mawer came in. Old Margaret Brompton buried.

9 September 1764

The house party, shortly to disperse, attends both church services. At some time that Sunday there is also a funeral, that of Margaret, wife of Richard Brunton.

Monday 10 not very well all day, after breakfast Miss Robinson left us, after Tea Mrs Mawer and Miss came in.

Tuesday 11 I drank Tea at Mrs Mawer's, with Mrs Newsham and Miss Simpson, in the Eve Miss Mawer and I down Street at the Shops.

Wednesday 12 dull day, shower of rain in the Eve, the Bride Mrs Newsham and Miss Simpson, Mrs Mawer and Miss drank tea with us.

12 September 1764

Betty, the bride, had recently married Richmond grocer James Newsham. She became a close friend and companion of the Diarist.

Sept 13 Mrs Nichols drank tea with us, after tea Miss Mawer came in, rainey night.

Friday 14 dull day. Mama got a bad cold, Mrs Mawer and Miss came in after dinner, set an hour. Wet night.

14 September 1764

Poor Mama is laid low. She seems to occupy a room with a fireplace so she can be kept comfortable, if under the weather.

Saturday 15 Mama badly set in her own room all day. Mr Wilson and Mr Rumney came to consult with us aboute a house for Mr Wilson. He has got two or three rooms at William Morgotroy['s] for the present. Mr Wilson stay'd all night with us. Miss Robinson came to dinner, in the Eve Mrs Mawer came in.

15 September 1764

Mr Wilson's arrival changed the Diarist's life, which came to revolve largely around the school which he and his wife established. William Morgotroy was a market gardener who used some of the land attached to Bowes Hall to grow his produce. He seems also to have been the tenant of part of that rambling complex, some of which could be used as schoolrooms. He also had a smallholding at St Nicholas, the ancient house on the edge of Richmond on the Brompton Road, and here kept cows from which he supplied Richmond residents with milk.

Sunday 16 disagreeable day, wind and rain, set in Mamas room too. Mr Wilson and Miss Robinson left us before dinner. My sister wrot to Nanny Smith. Mrs and Miss Mawer.

16 September 1764

The Diarist keeps her mother company while she is unwell, the fire kept burning in her room would be a comfort on a 'disagreeable day'. Miss Robinson must have been back again. The Sister, the family letter-writer, who seems only to have been around at weekends, corresponded with their sister-in-law in London.

Monday 17 Cold wind and rain. We had Sally Bowes and her two Children to drink Tea, in the Eve Mrs M and Miss.

17 September 1764

Sally Bowes was James Redhead's daughter, her children Elizabeth and Sarah were aged 2 and 5 months, so this must have been an atypical tea party!

Tuesday 18 I went in to Mrs Mawer's in the Morn, she is sating for her Picture. At 2 o'clock I went to Mrs Sandbridge's funeral. Dr Pringle came home with me and drank tea, Mrs Readhead came in and set an hour.

18 September 1764

Hannah Mawer is following her daughter's example in having her portrait painted, so they must have been pleased with how Henry Pickering had portrayed Bridget. This is a period when those of middle rank socially were beginning to acquire portraits. The parish register entry for the burial has Mrs Sandbirch as a 'widow a papist'. Dr Pringle seems often to persuade the Diarist to attend the funeral of one of his Roman Catholic patients, and returned home with the Diarist after the service.

Sept 19 very fine day, Miss Mawer and I down Street in the Morn at the Painter's to se his Pictures. After dinner I went to Mr Blackbourns to solicit for Mr Wilson but Miss Blackburn is engaged to Miss Johnson. Mrs Mawer and Miss drank Tea with us.

<u>*19 September 1764*</u>

Henry Pickering seems to have set himself up in a Richmond shop to display his paintings in the hope of attracting further commissions. This is an important piece of new information about how such peripatetic artists promoted their work. Revd Francis Blackburne, the rector of Richmond, lived in the large old rectory behind the parish church. His daughter Jane would later marry a clergyman who shared her father's Unitarian leanings. The Diarist's spelling of the Blackburne surname is unusually inconsistent for her, though typical for the period.

Thursday 20 pleasant morning, Miss Mawer and I had a walk to St. Martin's: nobody at home.

Friday 21 fine day, Mr Wilson drank Tea and Supped with us. Mrs Mawer and Miss came in for half an hour in the Eve. Two Miss Theakstons cal'd.

<u>*21 September 1764*</u>

Dorothy and Helen, daughters of Marmaduke Theakston of St Martin's, would later attend the Wilsons' school. The family had been out when the Diarist and Bridget Mawer had called the previous day.

Saturday 22 at Mrs Mawer's in the Morn. Mr and Mrs Wilson drank tea and Suped with us. I walk'd down Street with Miss Mawer and the Painter. A Serjeant in the Militia buried.

<u>*22 September 1764*</u>

Mr and Mrs Wilson are spending several days enjoying the Diarist's hospitality as they set up their school. It would seem that Henry Pickering had also obtained lodgings in Frenchgate. The funeral was that of John Dowson, described in the parish register as a 'serjeant in the Richmondshire Militia', the Diarist and the parish clerk both using the spelling current in Georgian times.

Sunday 23 at Church in the Morn. Miss Mawer came in after dinner. Mr and Mrs Wilson drank tea and Supd with us. Badly in the pain in my face.

Monday 24 the Militia comeing in to be exercised for a month. The Beast Fair, my sister got a letter from Miss Fanny Emerson in the Eve. Mrs Mawer and Miss came in, fine weather.

24 September 1764

The North York Militia mustered in Richmond each year, causing a conspicuous temporary increase in population. Richmond's ancient Rood Fair was originally held on the eve of and the feast day of the Holy Rood, or Cross, on 13 and 14 September. When the national calendar changed in 1754, Richmond corporation amended the Rood Fair dates to the 24 and 25 September. Cattle were sold on the first day as part of the jamboree of trading which took place then, hence the term 'Beast Fair' today, and 'the fair day' tomorrow.

Sept 25 the fair day, Fine Morn, down Street after dinner at Miss Dixon's. Old Mr Allen drank tea with us, in the Eve Miss Mawer and Mr and Mrs Wilson came in.

Sept 26 very fine day. I drank tea at Mrs Panton's with Mrs and Miss Strickland. A man burid, his name Foster. I went into Mrs Mawer's in the Eve for half an hour.

26 September 1764

James Forster was an innholder. As a market town, Richmond had a large number of inns and many of the licensees became prominent figures in the town. The Diarist knew several innholders well.

Thursday 27 rain and wind. Nanny washing. Mrs Wilson supd with us, after Supper I set an hour at Mrs Mawer's.

27 September 1764

Mrs Wilson was one of the few friends who stayed to eat with 'us', the Diarist's household.

Friday 28 very cold, in the afternoon we had Betty Tayler and her little girl. Mama and I at prayers in the Morn. In the Eve Mrs Mawer and Miss.

28 September 1764

Mama seems to have liked the extra litany included in the service of Morning Prayer on Fridays. This entry is unusual in not being chronological.

Saturday 29 extremely cold, rain and snow, in the Morn. Claping and dyeing, Mama and I drank Tea at Mrs Mawer's. Wheat at the market today 6s. 6d. a bushel. Beef and mutton 3d. a pd, a loyn of veal sold for 4s.

29 September 1764

Such unseasonably early snow as this was worth noting, as were the food prices. The day was Michaelmas, the Feast of St Michael the Archangel, a Quarter Day, when agricultural rents were paid, and so a traditional time of settling up. 'Claping' was a dialect word for smoothing yarn or laundered items.

Sunday 30 at Church in the Morn, rain all day. I drank tea with Mrs Wilson. Mr Wilson came with me and set til bedtime. After dinner Mrs Readhead and Miss Mawer came in.

October 1 very fine day, ironing in the Morn, at 3 o'clock Miss Bell Emerson arrived to make some stay with us. In the Eve Mrs Mawer and Miss came in, Mr P. came in for half an hour.

1 October 1764

Isabel Emerson, the second-oldest cousin, would stay in Richmond for five weeks, though the reason why does not become clear. The mysterious 'Mr P' might have been a potential suitor of hers.

Tuesday 2 Ironing in the Morn, very fine day. Mr P. drank tea with us, recivd a letter from Nanny Smith.

2 October 1764

Letters from Nanny Smith in London, whose husband Layton, the Diarist's brother, was in the Fleet Prison for debt, are unlikely ever to have brought good news. The sending to London of 'certificates' a few days later may have been a response to this letter.

Wednesday 3 fine day. Mr and Mrs Eubank drunk tea with us. In the Eve Mrs Mawer and Miss came in.

Thursday 4 Miss Bell and I down Street in the Morning at Miss Dixon's. Blustering wind, Dr. Pringle, Mrs Mawer and Miss drank tea with us, in the Eve Mrs Panton call'd to se Miss Emerson, Mrs Wilson came in.

4 October 1764

The presence of Bell Emerson is attracting several visitors to the house.

Friday 5 fine day, Miss Emerson and Mrs Colingwood walk'd to Mr. Lodg[e']s, in the Evening Mama, Miss Bell and I set an hour at Mrs Mawer's.

5 October 1764

Mr Lodge's was St Trinian's, a handsome Georgian house near Easby occupied successively by a number of 'upwardly mobile' families. George Lodge was an elderly gentleman and would die a year later and be succeeded by his son Ralph.

Saturday 6 after Tea Miss Bell and I walk'd down Street in the Eve. Mr and Mrs Wilson came in.

Sunday 7 Mama, Miss Bell and I at Church in the Morn, Miss Bell in the afternoon. Very fine day, in the Eve Mrs Mawer and Miss came in.

Monday 8 very bad day, my sister wrote to A. Nickhols by Fanny Cowling. In the Eve Miss Mawer came in.

8 October 1764

A member of another Richmond family, the Cowlings, was saving postage by taking the sister's letter to Alice Nichols in London.

Octo 9 Miss Pye gave us a call. Miss Bell and I maid a visit to n(e)ice Robinson's, along with Mr and Mrs Newsam, a shower of rain. Mrs Mawer and Miss came in in the Eve.

9 October 1764

Miss Pye was friendly with Dr Pringle, and may have been a Roman Catholic. Bell's presence is still generating a flurry of social activities.

Wednesday 10 I wrote to my Uncle Smith with the Certificates, my Sister wrot to Miss Emerson. Mama, Miss Emerson and I drunk Tea at Mrs Mawer's.

10 October 1764

Uncle Thomas Smith in London has certificates sent to him on several occasions, but they are never explained.

Thursday 11 Miss Bell and I walk'd up to Dr. Pringle's to se Mrs James and Miss Pye. Miss Mawer, Miss Bell and I went upon the field to se the Militia Exercise. After we got home it came on a very heavy rain. Dr. Pringle, Mrs James and Miss Pye drank tea with us, in the Eve Mrs Mawer and Miss.

11 October 1764

The three younger women were interested in watching the young militia officers, in their handsome red uniforms, take part in the training exercises. The scheme worked, as an invitation would shortly arrive for their forthcoming ball!

Friday 12 very rainy Morning, better in the afternoon, Miss Bell and I maid a visit to Mrs Newsam, Mrs Mawer and Miss in the Eve.

Octor 13 fine day, Miss Pye in the Morning she engaged Mama to drink Tea at the Dr's. Mrs James sent her Chaise for us, in the Eve Miss Bell and I went in to Mrs Mawer's. An invitation from the Officers to a ball next Thursday night.

13 October 1764

This entry is particularly interesting as it provides details of how people were invited to take tea. Mrs James is mentioned just briefly, but she must have been a well-to-do lady to have her own chaise, which was used to transport Mama across Richmond from Frenchgate to Dr Pringle's house in Newbiggin.

Sunday 14 fine morning, Miss Bell and I at Church, Miss Pye set with us. After dinner we set an hour with Mrs Panton at her new lodgings, Mrs Wagit's, Mr, Mrs and Miss Ctrickland [Strickland] drank tea with us.

14 October 1764

*The Mawers' friend Mrs Panton, apparently a widow, seems
typically to have rented her accommodation in Richmond. The
lady with whom she took lodgings, Ann Waggett, who was also a
widow, lived at the top of Frenchgate on the west side.*

Monday 15 Miss Pye, Miss Bell and I walk'd to the field to see the
men, very cold, down Street at the Shops. Miss Bell and I maid
a visit to Mrs Panton, we met with Mrs Simpson there, in the
Evening we all went into Mrs Mawer's.

15 October 1764

*Watching the Militia train seems to have been a morning activity.
Mrs Panton's new abode is still attracting those curious to inspect
it. Mrs Simpson was the wife of a prosperous mercer.*

Tuesday 16 Mrs Mawer and Miss drank tea with us.

Octor 17 tolerable day, rain in the Evening, Miss Bell and I drank
Tea at Mrs Waynes. Miss Pye spent the afternoon with Mama and
Sister, after super Miss Bell and I at Mrs Mawer's.

17 October 1764

*Mrs Wayne was the wife of apothecary Christopher Wayne,
a prominent alderman who served three terms as Mayor of
Richmond.*

Thursday 18 Miss Bell and I at the Ball, we danced 20 couples,
Miss Bell and Mr C. Readshaw, Mr R. Brockell and my Self. In the
Eve Mrs Mawer came in.

18 October 1764

*Bell Emerson's desirable dancing partner at the militia officers'
ball was Caleb Readshaw, a member of an old-established
Richmond family of merchants who had, about 1740, built a fine
Georgian town house, The Grove, at the bottom of Frenchgate;
unusually for Georgian Richmond, it was built in brick. Several
generations of the family were confusingly called Caleb and
Cuthbert. The Diarist's partner, Ralph Brockell, was the 29-year-
old scion of another well-established Richmond family.*

Friday 19 fine day, Miss Bell and I at prayers. Miss Pay drunk tea with us. Miss Mawer came in, after Supper at Mrs Mawer's.

19 October 1764

Miss Pay here is probably meant to be Miss Pye.

Saturday 20 Miss Bell and I down Street at the Shops. Mr Wilson drank tea with us.

Sunday 21 Miss Bell and I at Church Morn and Eve. We drank tea with Miss Dixon. Wind and some Showers of rain, in the Eve Mrs Mawer and Miss.

21 October 1764

Bell Emerson dutifully attends church, twice this Sunday and also the previous Friday, but the girls had had a visit to the shops on the market day in-between.

Monday 22 Wind and rain in the morning, a tolerable afternoon. Miss Bell and I maid a visit to Mrs Close. After Supper we set an hour at Mrs Mawer.

22 October 1764

Elizabeth Close was the younger wife of John Close, a member of an influential Richmond family. John and Elizabeth would in a few months time move with their young family out of the town into the large house at Easby owned by the Smith family.

Tuesday 23 very cold, Mr and Mrs Wilson drunk tea with us, in the eve Miss Dixon cald to ask us to put in to a raffle for flower'd lawn Aprons and ruffles 2s. 6d. a lot, Miss Bell and me are in, after Supper Mrs Mawer came in.

23 October 1764

The Diarist was not only a good customer of Faith Dixon, who had a drapery and haberdashery shop on the High Row in Richmond, but she was also a friend. Aprons in flowered lawn were a desirable decorative item of clothing, not a utilitarian protection, and ruffles were similarly worn over dresses.

Octo 24 very fine day, Miss Mawer, Miss Pye, Miss Bell and I walk'd to Love Lain, and drank tea. Mrs Mawer drank tea with Mama and Sister.

24 October 1764

Love Lane runs from Easby east towards what is now called Red House Farm, but used to be Love Lane Farm, beyond which in Georgian times there was a fashionable beauty spot on the bank of the river Swale. The Diarist's friend Betty Beautyment lived at the farm, and the younger group of ladies would take tea with her. The Diarist's sister apparently preferred the elderly company of Mama and Mrs Mawer to a walk in the country.

Thursday 25 Cold wind, shower of snow. Miss Bell and I drunk tea at Mrs Colingwood's, after Supper we set an hour at Mrs Mawer's.

Friday 26 very bad day, Wind, rain and snow, in the Eve Mrs Mawer and Miss came in.

26 October 1764

The Diarist, always a keen observer of the weather, is presumably disappointed at the unseasonably early start to winter this autumn.

27 Miss Bell and I down Street at the Shops. I got a new Stuff Gown at Mr Simpson's 1s. 3d. a yard. We drunk tea at Mrs Mawer's. Mr Wilson in the Eve.

27 October 1764

It sounds as though the Diarist and her cousin browsed among many of the shops in the central area of the town. Perhaps Bell persuaded the Diarist to treat herself to a new gown, in a warm material, at the shop of her friend Thomas Simpson, a mercer or dealer in good quality fabrics.

Sunday 28 Miss Bell and I at Church, Morn and Evening. Miss Pye din'd and drank tea with us. Mrs Wilson in the Evening.

Monday 29 Mrs Panton and Miss Mawer maid us a Morning Visit. Miss Bell and I maid a Visit at Mrs Strickland, to Miss Charlotte who is thust come from France, Mrs Mawer and Miss.

29 October 1764

Charlotte Strickland was the youngest child of Richmond Jacobite Roger Strickland, and his wife Catherine Scrope of Danby. They sent their children to be educated in France, where Roman Catholic boarding schools catered specifically for the children of British recusants. At 16, Charlotte had just finished her schooling there. She seems to have had rather a sad life, having suffered a bad attack of smallpox as a child of 5, she may have been scarred on the face. Certainly she did not marry, and after living with various relatives she became a pensioner in the house of the English Canonesses of the Holy Sepulchre in Belgium, where she lived until her death in 1804.

Tuesday 30 Mrs Deighton drank Tea with us. I recvd a letter from Mrs Huggans, one inclosd for Mr F. Allen. In the Eve Miss Bell and I at the Mawers.

Octr 31 very Stormy day, rain and snow, Peggy Morland buried. Miss Mawer in the Eve.

31 October 1764

Another reference to the funeral of one of the ladies in the same social set, recorded in the parish register as 'Margaret Morley widow'.

Novr 1 Ironing in the Morn, in the afternoon Miss Mawer, Miss Bell and I at the raffle at Miss Dixon's. Miss Bell got the highest prize, a flowered lawn Apron, we got home to Tea. Mrs Mawer and Miss set til 9 o'clock. Wet night.

1 November 1764

Ironing took up part of two days this week. Bell Emerson would doubtless have suitable gowns to set off the desirable flowered lawn apron, the top prize in the somewhat expensive raffle subscribed to a few days earlier.

Novr 2 finish'd my Ironing. We all drank tea at Mrs Mawers. Mama recvd a letter from my Uncle Smith with two inclosd from Layton to himself.

2 November 1764

The correspondence received by Mama from her brother-in-law,
the London lawyer Thomas Smith, and her son, the debtor Layton
Smith, seems to have brought news so traumatic that the Diarist
was unable to pen entries for four days.

Saturday 3rd to Tuesday 6th November – no entries

Wednesday 7 I went home with Cousin Bell Emerson to Winston,
and stayd two months.

7 November 1764

The Diarist must have retrospectively made this entry, the only
one between 2 November 1764 and 4 January 1765. She does
not enlighten us about the reason for the mysterious and prolonged
stay in Winston. Bell Emerson, who had been staying in Richmond
with the Diarist since the 1 October, would seem to have taken her
back home with her, possibly to comfort her, either in her distress
due to the London news, or possibly because she was suffering an
illness. There is no indication of where Mama was during this
period, did she also go away?

Thursday 8 November to Friday 4 January – no entries

Jan. 5 1765 I return'd from Winston, a thick dark day, in the
Evening Mrs Mawer and Miss, Mr and Mrs Wilson came in to
welcome me home.

5 January 1765

The two Mawers and the two Wilsons visit in the evening to
welcome the Diarist home after her two-month absence from
Richmond. There is no mention of either her sister or Mama
similarly welcoming her back.

Sunday 6 Mrs and Miss Mawer drank Tea with us.

Monday 7 I walk'd down to the Green to deliver a Picture to
Mrs York that I brought from Winston.

7 January 1765

The picture must have been quite small if the Diarist could carry
it down to the Yorke mansion on the Green. It is not clear which

*Mrs Yorke was the intended recipient. The wife of the then owner
of the estate, Sophia Yorke, was a young woman with a small
baby, Sophia Anne, who sadly would die a few months later. Her
mother-in-law Anne was an elderly lady in her 60s who was also
living there.*

Tuesday 8 Mrs Readhead drank Tea with us, rainey thick weather.
Dr Pringle and Miss Nendike marry'd.

8 January 1765

*The Diarist's entry is enigmatic as to whether or not she attended
the wedding of her friend the Roman Catholic doctor, James
Pringle, to Rosa, the daughter of his colleague apothecary John
Nandike.*

Wednesday 9 Mama and I drank Tea at Mrs Mawers. A Child buried.

9 January 1765

*The child buried was Joseph the son of Francis Hopps, a
cordwainer (shoemaker). The Diarist possibly knew him as a
shopkeeper.*

Thursday 10 in the Eve Mr Wilson and Miss Mawer came in.

Friday 11 writeing to Winston, after dinner down Street get[t]ing
something at the Shops. In the Eve Mrs Wilson and Miss Mawer,
Miss and I playd at Cribbage til 10 o'clock.

11 January 1765

*The evening spent playing cribbage is a rare reference to a home-
based leisure activity.*

Saturday 12 Mrs Mawer and Miss drank Tea with us.

Sunday 13 very fine clear day, at Church in the Morn. Maid a visit
to Mrs Pringle the Bride. Mrs Wilson and Miss Mawer came in in
the Eve.

13 January 1765

*The pleasant winter weather encouraged a walk to see the new
Mrs Pringle in her fine Georgian house in Newbiggin, which her
husband James had recently built.*

Jan 14 in the Morn Mrs Panton and Miss Mawer cald, they are going to Raby. Mrs Mawer sent to ask Mama and me to drink Tea with her and her Son Key. After Supper they came and set with us. Mr T. Cornforth chose Mayor.

14 January 1765

This entry contains the first reference to Mama since the Diarist's return from Winston nine days before. The Mawer family's uncharacteristic behaviour is intriguing; did Kay Mawer have to take over companion duties so that Bridget could accompany Mrs Panton to Raby Castle? The new mayor for that year, Thomas Cornforth, came from a prosperous Teesdale family well known to the Diarist. He was a young man to hold such office, only 31, and had recently moved to Richmond to undertake legal and financial work for Sir Lawrence Dundas. He had paid to be admitted into the Company of Mercers, Grocers and Haberdashers in order to become a freeman of Richmond and thus eligible to serve on the Corporation. He would again serve as mayor in 1776 and 1786.

Jan 15 I sent my letter by the Post to Cousn Bell. I recd a letter from Winston. The Mayor's Feast.

15 January 1765

There is a lot of correspondence flying back and forth to Winston, including a letter to cousin Bell sent by expensive postage. The new mayor was hosting the corporation's ceremonial meal immediately on taking office.

Jan 16 in the Evening Mrs Mawer came in.

Thursday 17 got a letter from Winston returnd an answer. Makeing Mama's Shifts. Mrs Wilson in the Eve.

17 January 1765

The shifts being made for Mama were undergarments, probably nightgowns.

Friday 18 after dinner I set half an hour with Mrs Mawer.

Jan 19 in the Even Mr and Mrs Wilson came in.

Sunday 20 a fine clear day, at Church Morn and Eve. Mrs Mawer drank tea with us.

Monday 21 a dark wet day. At one o'clock Miss Jenny and Miss Fanny Emerson came to go to the Mayor's Ball. After dinner Miss Mawer came in, she is thust got home from Raby Castle at 7 o'clock. Miss Emersons and I went to the Town Hall. We danc'd 26 couples. We got home at 2 o'clock.

21 January 1765

Bridget Mawer calls as soon as she returns from Raby Castle. After all that recent correspondence between the Diarist and her Winston cousins, the two younger ones arrive to attend the Mayor's Ball. This highly successful and exciting social occasion continued into the early hours, and with the large number of twenty-six couples dancing, must have been quite a squash in the Town Hall, recently erected as an Assembly Room!

Jan 22 a dark, thick day. Miss Emersons went home in the morning. Mr and Mrs Wilson drunk tea with us. After Supper I went in to Mrs Mawer's.

22 January 1765

The Emersons, as a Teesdale family, would know well the new mayor, Thomas Cornforth. They had come especially for the ball and return home immediately after.

Jan 23 in the Evening Mrs and Miss Mawer came in.

Jan 24 rain all day, bad in a cold.

Friday 25 Mama and I drank tea at Mrs Mawer's.

Saturday 26 down Street at Miss Dixon's, drank Tea with Mrs Newsam. Mr Bently paid us 15s. for Layton's books and return'd them he could not dispose of.

26 January 1765

The books belonged to Layton Smith, the Diarist's brother, a debtor in the Fleet Prison in London.

Sunday 27 a fine clear day at Church Morn and Evening. Mrs Mawer and Miss, Mama and I drank tea at Mr Wilson's.

Monday 28 fine day, Frost, in the Eve Mrs Mawer and Mrs Readhead came in, the Revd. Mr Nichols set an hour.

28 January 1765

Christopher Nichols, a clergyman serving as a curate in Cambridge, was spending the first months of the year back with his family in Richmond. He would visit the Diarist four times during this period.

Jan. 29 Frost, in the Garden an hour. Mrs Wilson spent the Eve with us. Miss Mawer came in.

29 January 1765

Despite noting that there was frost, the Diarist has still spent an hour in the garden which suggests there must be a strong reason for gardening on such cold days.

Jan. 30. Frost, in the Garden again, Miss Strickland drank Tea with us, my Sister writing to Nanny Smith. It is to go by our maid's brother, he goes for London tomorrow.

30 January 1765

The sister's letter to Nanny Smith may have been to tell her of the 15s which had been obtained by selling her husband's books, though this sum presumably did not go very far towards his debts. This is another example of letters being taken to London by someone travelling there, instead of paying expensive postage. Was the brother of maids Nanny and Betty going to take up a job in service in London?

Jan. 31 Frost. Dr., Mrs Pringle the brid[e] and Miss Elliker the bride maid drank Tea with us. Mama and I set an hour at Mrs Mawer's, Mr and Mrs Wilson spent the Eve with us.

31 January 1765

The reference to Miss Elliker, who does not appear otherwise in the diary, gives another nice snippet of information about Georgian weddings, that the term bridesmaid was used.

Feb. 1 Mr and Mrs Wilson drank Tea with us. Two Funerals, Nanny Walker and Peggy Wells.

1 February 1765

The Wilsons are currently frequent visitors. The parish register shows the burial entries as 'the wife of Richard Walker cooper', and 'Margaret Wells'.

Saturday 2 Cold day. Butter 10d. a p[oun]d. Betty Beautyment drank Tea with us, after Supper I went in to Mrs Mawer's.

2 February 1765

Butter would be scarce at this time of year when cows gave little milk, so presumably Betty Beautyment had been able to sell all she had brought to Richmond's Saturday market. Afterwards she was able to take tea with the Diarist, whereas the Diarist often visited her farmhouse down Love Lane at Easby when out for a walk.

Sunday 3 Frost and snow. Mama and I drank Tea at Mrs Mawer's, Mrs Readhead there. After dinner I set half an hour at Mr Wilson's, in the Evening Mr and Mrs Wilson came in.

3 February 1765

The fact that there was frost and snow suggests that all the visits were made unusually close to home, in other words all the people mentioned were living in very close proximity to one another, hence the inference that all lived in the rambling Bowes Hall which would have provided several apartments.

Monday 4 Frost and Snow, Mrs Mawer & Mrs Readhead drank Tea with us.

Feb. 5 Frost and snow. Miss Wycleff and two Miss Rumneys from Mrs Wilson's drank Tea with us. Two Funerals John Walker's wife, and Mary Mafham [sic], both liv'd in Bargate. My Sister got a letter from Nanny Smith.

5 February 1765

The first indication that the Wilsons have succeeded in recruiting some pupils to their school. 'Miss Wycleff' was almost certainly a young member of the family of Wycliffe, of which there were several

branches in and around Richmond. Thomas Wycliffe Esquire of
Richmond, whose memorial inscription in the chancel of Kirkby
Ravensworth church claims that he was the last male descendant
of the reformer Wycliffe, died in 1821. He had two sisters Lucy
and Catherine, one of whom could have attended the Wilsons'
school. The two Miss Rumneys are presumably related to, perhaps
the daughters of, the Mr Rumney who arrived with Mr Wilson
when he first announced his intention to start a school. Several
people of the name Rumney were schoolmasters in the Newcastle
and Alnwick areas, where Mr Wilson did some of his recruitment.
The reference to the funerals of people living in Bargate is a rare
reference to an 'address' in Richmond. Bargate was then considered
an unfashionable area, leading as it did to Richmond's industrial
suburb, The Green. The parish registers record the burials of
'Margaret wife of John Walker', and of 'Mary Maugham ideot'.

Feb. 6 Frost, we got the Chimney sweepd. Mama and I drank tea at
Mrs Wilson's. After Supr I went in to Mrs M's.

6 February 1765

The reference to having 'the' chimney swept suggests that it was
the main one of the house, which would be used for cooking and
therefore lit every day of the year. We have inferred that Mama's
room was the only other one where a fire was sometimes available
for comfort and warmth.

Thursday 7 Frost. Eppey Beautyment and her Cousin drank Tea
with us, in the Eve Mrs Mawer came in. About 6 o'clock we were
greatly alarm'd by the Fire bell, in a little time we were inform'd
that Mrs Jane Geldard's house was in fire, by 10 o'clock the greatest
part of it was consumed, but by the calmness of the night and
good assistance it was prevented from doing any farther damage.
Mr Harrison's only Child, a son, was buried.

7 February 1765

Possibly the unfortunate Jane Geldard had not had her chimney
swept. She had succeeded both her father and her mother as
licensee of the 'Griffin Inn', then a timber-framed building on the
site of no. 6 Market Place. The townsfolks' response to the ringing
of the Fire Bell from the tower of Holy Trinity Chapel in the
market place was clearly inadequate in dealing with this major
house fire, and a few weeks later Sir Lawrence Dundas of Aske

Hall presented Richmond corporation with its first fire engine
ready to deal with such calamities in the future.

Friday 8 not very well, set in Mama's room all day, in the Evening Mrs Wilson came in.

8 February 1765

The use of Mama's room as a sickbay suggests that it
could be heated and made more comfortable than other
areas of the house.

Feb. 9 I got down stairs. I recd a letter from Cousen Bell Emerson, in the Eve Miss Mawer came in.

9 February 1765

The Diarist's household accommodation is clearly on at least
two floors. This is significant, because many Georgian lodgings
consisted of a single floor in a house, rather than an apartment.

Sunday 10 Rain. Very bad, set in Mama's Room all day, in the Eve Miss Mawer and Matty Beauly came in.

10 February 1765

If the Diarist spent the day in her Mama's room, it is testament
to the intimacy of her friendship with Miss Mawer and Matty
Beauly that they should visit her in one of her home's 'private'
rooms upstairs.

Feb. 11 got down Stairs, Mrs Readhead set half an hour. Mr, Mrs Wilson and Miss Wycleff came in.

Feb. 12 fine clear day, set in Mama's Room, Miss M came in.

12 February 1765

Miss M is Bridget Mawer, a good friend who keeps visiting the
invalid.

Feb. 13 got down Stairs, Miss Mawer drank Tea with us.

Feb. 14 Cold day, some Showers of Snow. Mama and I drank Tea at Mrs Mawers. Our maid Nanny gon away, we have got her Sister Betty to stay with us til May day upon trial.

14 February 1765

The maid Nanny's sister Betty seems to have been a successful appointment, as she was kept on after May Day.

Friday 15 Mrs Newsham sent to drink Tea with us, she had not been half an hour when she was sent for home, her Father is ill. Mr and Mrs Wilson drank Tea with us, and set til bedtime. Mrs & Miss Mawer came in.

15 February 1765

Young Mrs Newsam was within a few months of giving birth to her first child, so having to rush away to her family home must have been very traumatic.

Feb. 16 Recvd a letter from Miss Bell Emerson, return'd an answer. Mrs Mawer sent in for me to drink tea.

16 February 1765

Isabel, the second eldest Emerson cousin, is a frequent correspondent.

Sunday 17 Snow all the Morn. Got a very bad cold and sore throat, after tea Mrs and Miss Mawer came in.

17 February 1765

The poor Diarist is having a bout of illness this month. She has scarcely recovered from a previous spell a week ago before going down with this bad cold.

Monday 18 Frost and a covering of Snow, the Revd. Mr Nichols and Mrs Readhead drank tea with us. Two Funerals, an old Woman her name Ward, and a Girl of John Thwates. After Supper Miss M came in.

18 February 1765

The parish registers record the funerals as being of 'Anne Ward widow' and 'Jane daughter of John Thwaites'.

Tuesday 19 Frost, a Company of Foot Soldiers came in to Town in there march [?] from Scotland to London. They march out tomorrow Morning. Mr and Mrs Wilson drank tea with us and spent the Evening.

19 February 1765

The soldiers arrive in three contingents over four days, each company staying just one night to allow the inns where they were billeted to cope with the numbers.

Ash wednesday Feb. 20 Frost. Another Company of Soldiers came in. Mama and I drank tea at Mr Wilson's, in the Evening Miss Mawer came in with her work.

20 February 1765

Ash Wednesday is the first day of Lent, a season of forty days before the moveable feast of Easter. Was Bridget Mawer doing needlework, such as lace making?

Thursday 21 Frost, in the morn I went down Street, paid Mrs Dixon's note, got 4 pocket handkerchiefs. In the Eve, Mrs Readhead sat an hour with us. After Supper Mrs Mawer and Miss came in.

21 February 1765

The haberdashery shop owner Faith Dixon has also allowed the Diarist to shop on credit.

Friday 22 frost, the last division of Soldiers came in. We got 6 load of Coals at 10d. a load. Mrs and Miss Mawer drank tea with us, in the Evening the Revd. Mr Nicholls set half an hour with us.

22 February 1765

It is interesting to note that various members of the Nicholls family seem to be regular visitors to the Diarist at present.

Saturday 23 The Soldiers marched oute of Town, Mrs Nicholls drank tea with us. In the Eve I went into Mrs Mawer's.

Sunday 24 at Church Morn and Eve, Mama got a letter from Mrs Smith from London to acquaint her that she had heard from her Son, that he was thust recovered from a fever. Mama and I drank tea at Mrs Readhead's, Mrs and Miss Mawer there, my Sister wrote to Betty Nicholls. Mr and Mrs Wilson spent the Eve with us. Miss Mawer came in.

Did the post boy work on Sundays, or had someone brought the letter from London earlier and Mama just disclosed it? Ann Smith was married to the Diarist's brother Layton, a debtor in the Fleet Prison, where he must have caught the fever that he had just recovered from. He is known to have looked after his fellow prisoners when they were ill.

Monday 25 I drank tea at George Hutchinson's, after Mrs Mawer sat an hour with us.

25 February 1765

George Hutchinson and his wife were a couple with a 4-year-old son, also George, and they lived in Millgate. George senior was a soldier in the Durham Militia, a unit which was based in Richmond for much of the 1760s, and which had for a time the astronomer William Herschel in its band.

Tuesday 26 I recvd a letter from Mrs Huggans. After Supper Mrs Mawer came in, Miss is gon to Gainford.

26 February 1765

Bridget Mawer's trip to Gainford is a preliminary before she and her mother left Richmond to settle there in the May.

Feb. 27 A covering of Snow. I paid James Crain in full for Coals 6s. which is 8d. more than his dues. Mama and I drank tea at Mrs Mawer's.

27 February 1765

After such a prolonged cold spell, the Diarist has been fortunate to be able to stock up on coal, and she is doubtless wise to keep well in with James Crain the coal merchant.

Thursday 28 Cold day, se nobody but Miss Mawer in the Eve.

28 February 1765

An unusually quiet day in the Diarist's normally full social life.

Friday Mar 1 at prayers in the Morning, very Cold. After dinner walk'd down Street with Miss Mawer, call'd at Matty's as I came home. After Super Mrs Mawer sent for me to set with them.

1 March 1765

Attendance at the Friday service of Morning Prayer which included an extra litany. Bridget Mawer has returned from her stay in Gainford.

Saturday 2 Cold day, wind and rain, writeing to Miss B. Emerson. After dinner Mrs Readhead sat an hour with us. In the Eve Miss Mawer came in. I went in there after Super.

2 March 1765

The Diarist and Bell Emerson are keeping up their correspondence. Bridget Mawer visits the Diarist, and the Diarist visits the Mawers on the same day.

Sunday 3 very fine day, badly all day, not at Church. After dinner Mrs Mawer, Miss and Mrs Nicholls came in. Mr and Mrs Wilson spent the Eve with us.

3 March 1765

The Diarist is still in poor health. It is rare for her to miss church on Sundays. At least she had plenty of company.

Monday 4 tolerable day. Mrs Mawer and Miss drank Tea with us.

March 5 Violent Stormey day, Wind and Snow. Mr and Mrs Wilson drank tea with us, in the Eve, Miss Wycliffe came in for me to teach her to nett. After Supper I went into Mrs Mawer's.

5 March 1765

Was the Diarist teaching the Wilsons' pupil Miss Wycliffe to knit, or to make lace net, possibly by tatting? This pupil would become a regular visitor, presumably learning the etiquette of tea drinking as part of her education.

Wednesday 6 Betty washing. Miss Wycliffe drank tea with us. In the Eve Mrs Wilson and Mrs Readhead came in. After Supper Miss Mawer came in.

6 March 1765

Despite the poor weather, the maid has to see to the domestic washing.

March 7 *Frost*. I finishd my Nett Hood. In the Eve we had Miss Wycliffe and Mrs Mawer. After supper Miss Mawer. Very indifferent in a pain in my face and head.

7 March 1765

The Diarist's expertise in the craft of 'netting' enabled her not only to make herself a nett hood, but also to teach young women the skill.

Friday 8 badly in my head, Mama and I drank tea at Mrs Mawer's. In the Eve Mrs Wilson and Miss Wycliffe came in.

Saturday 9 Rain. Mr, Mrs Wilson and Miss Wycliffe drank tea with us. After Supper I went in to Mrs Mawer's.

Sunday 10 at Church in the Morn. Cold wet day, after dinner I sat an hour at Mr Wilson's. In the Eve Mrs Mawer and Miss came in.

10 March 1765

At least the Diarist was well enough to attend church this Sunday.

Monday 11 *Snow*. Ironing in the Morn, Miss Wycliffe drank tea with us. In the Eve Miss Mawer came in, I went in there after Supper.

March 12 Ironing in the Morn. Mr and Mrs Wilson drank tea with us and spent the Eve. Mrs Readhead and Miss Mawer came in and sat an hour.

12 March 1765

The washing that had been done resulted in three days of ironing.

March 13 Miserable day, both rain and snow, finishd my Ironing. Miss Wycliffe drank tea with us, in the Eve Miss Mawer came in.

March 14 Wind with some Showers of Snow, Mama and I drank tea at Mrs Mawer's. A Child buried in the Smallpox. In the Eve Mrs Wilson came in.

14 March 1765

The child who had died of smallpox was Anne, the daughter of William Ingleby, who lived next door to Dr Pringle in Newbiggin.

Friday 15 Cold and Windy. Miss Wycliffe drank tea with us. In the Eve Mrs Wilson and Miss Mawer came in.

March 16 very Cold. I sent a letter to Miss Bell Emerson. Mama received a present of a cheese from Mrs Moor. Mr and Mrs Wilson drank tea with us, in the Eve Miss Mawer came in, after Super I went in.

16 March 1765

Again a letter to Isabel Emerson. Mama is the recipient of another edible present, this time a cheese, presumably from the widow of Revd James Moore in Arkengarthdale.

Sunday 17 Fine Clear day, at Church Morn and Eve. After dinner Mr Mrs Wilson and I had a walk til Church time. My Sister wrote to Miss Pye. Mama and I drank tea at Mr Wilson's. After Supper Mrs Mawer and Miss came in.

17 March 1765

The good day for the time of year prompts some fresh air, Mr Wilson does not seem to have enjoyed walking as often as the ladies. It would seem that the Wilsons joined the Diarist at church, at least for Evening Prayer.

Monday 18 Extreamly Cold, a thick covering of Snow, in the Eve rain. After tea Miss Wycliffe came, after Supper I went in to Mrs Mawer's.

March 19 a blustering Wind with showers of rain and hail. I got down Street to Mrs Dixon's to get some diaper to send to Winston. I got 6 yards at 9d. a yd.

19 March 1765

The diaper was a linen cloth, probably for napery. Obviously at this period it had to be supplied from Richmond, rather than Barnard Castle.

March 20 The Weather the same as yesterday. I paid Christopher Wright a shilling for a Common day's work. In the Eve Mrs Wilson and Miss Mawer came in.

20 March 1765

> *The Common Day's work was statute labour for the maintenance of roads which householders were obliged to provide. Statute labour could be directed to the new turnpike roads, as in this case, when work was being carried out on the Richmond to Gilling West and Richmond to Brompton-on-Swale roads. A shilling was the going rate for hiring a labourer to do the householder's duty.*

March 21 Rain and Wind. I drank Tea with Miss Mawer. Mary Kelley buried.

21 March 1765

> *The parish register records the burial of 'Mary Kelley widow'.*

Friday 22 at prayers in the Morn. After dinner Mrs Mawer sat an hour with us. Mr and Wilson drank Tea and Suped with us. Miss M came in.

March 23 Received a letter from Miss Bell Emerson with a very bad account of my uncle's health. After dinner I went down Street, call'd upon Mrs Panton and Mrs Simpson, bought half an ounce of Cotton for my Aunt at Miss Wayd's, 1s. 8d. an ounce. Drank Tea with Mrs Newsam, prodigious wind.

23 March 1765

> *Isabel, the eldest cousin still at home in Winston, and the frequent correspondent, writes to inform the Diarist of Revd John Emerson's illness. It would seem the letter also included the usual request for some drapery shopping in Richmond, this time requested by the Diarist's aunt Ann Emerson.*

Sunday 24 A shower of rain in the Morn, at Church Morn and Eve. Mrs Mawer and Miss, Mr and Mrs Wilson came in in the Eve.

Monday 25 March Finished Mama's Stocking, in the Eve Mrs Mawer and Miss sat an hour with us.

March 26 Excessive rain all day, drawing a pair of Ruffles to work. Mama and I drank Tea at Mrs Mawer's.

The Diarist is engaged in a lot of handicraft. Having completed the knitting of Mama's stocking, she immediately begins threadwork on ruffles, and also buys ribbons in a sale the next day.

March 27 Wind with some Showers of rain, in the Morn Miss Mawer and I walk'd down Street to Miss Wrather's. They are sel[l]ing up thear [sic] goods at prime cost, we got some ribbands. In the afternoon Mrs Panton gave us a Call, in the Eve Mrs Mawer and Miss came in.

March 28 The day much the same as yesterday. Writeing to Miss Bell Emerson. Mr Wilson and Mr Nicholls drank Tea with us. I went into Mrs Mawer's.

Bell Emerson will presumably be eager to hear the news of bargain ribbons.

Friday 29 The same weather. Mr and Mrs Wilson drank Tea with us, Mrs and Miss Mawer in the Eve.

Fair Day 30 Wind with some Showers, down Street for half an hour to buy fairings. Sent a letter and parcel to Winston. Mr and Mrs Wilson Supd with us. This morning dyed Miss Coats. After Supper I sat half an hour at Mrs Mawer's.

The Saturday before Palm Sunday was one of Richmond's ancient fairs, fairings being cheap souvenirs sold by visiting traders. Elizabeth Coats, who had earned her living as a skilled 'spinster' of yarn as well as being a single lady, was probably both a friend of the Diarist as well as one with whom she did business. The Diarist acted as a pallbearer at the funeral two days later, requiring the wearing of white hoods and gloves to hold the pall, which covered the coffin, off the ground.

March 31 Cold wind, rain in the Eve, at Church in the Morn. Mama and I drank Tea at Mrs Mawer's, Mrs Wilson and Miss Wycliffe there.

April 1 Cold wind with showers. At 4 o'clock I went to Miss Coatses Funeral to be a bearer, we had white hoods and gloves. In the Eve Mrs Mawer came in.

*The Diarist specifically tells us that she attended this funeral,
rather than referring to the event as someone having been buried.*

Tuesday 2 Cold wind, after dinner Mrs Mawer came in. After Tea
I went in there and sat tel 8 o'clock. Mr Ca[leb] Readshaw chose
Alderman. The Bells Rang, upon occasion. An Old Woman buried.

2 April 1765

*Bell Emerson's erstwhile dancing partner Caleb Readshaw was
very young to become an Alderman at about the age of 23. He
would be elected a very young mayor the following year, so he had
a meteoric rise to power in Richmond, doubtless due to his family's
influence. Presumably they also paid the bell-ringers. The burial
was of another widow, Margaret Russell.*

Wednesday 3 Cold with Showers, sent my letter to Winston. Mr and
Mrs Wilson drank Tea with us, Miss M came in.

Thursday 4 Cold with Showers, I recvd a letter from Miss Bell
Emerson with a melancholy account of her Father. We were
desired to order an Electuary from Mr Wayne which we did and
sent by the man. I went to Miss Wrather's to get some ribband for
Miss F. Emerson. After Supper I sat an hour at Mrs Mawer's.

4 April 1765

*Cousin Bell's letter gives a worse account of uncle John Emerson's
illness. However, Dr Wayne's potion seems to have been effective,
for not only was uncle much better ten days later, but he lived
another nine years. Again the letter asked for some shopping, this
time ribbons for Fanny, possibly to refresh either a bonnet or a
dress. Richmond drapers stocked more fashionable wares than
those in other northern towns.*

Good Friday 5 very fine day, Mama and I Church in the Morn.
After Eve prayers I had a walk to Easby with Mr and Mrs Medcalf,
Mr and Mrs Newsam. In the Eve Mrs Mawer and Miss came in,
rainey night.

5 April 1765

*Good Friday saw the Diarist at church twice, but the fine weather
drew her and two couples to walk to Easby after the second service.*

Saturday 6 Violent Wind with Showers of rain and hail. We got 10 load of coals at 10½d. a load. In the Eve Miss Mawer came in.

6 April 1765

The price of this delivery of coal has gone up slightly since the last delivery at the end of February.

April 7 Easter Sunday The weather the same as yesterday, at Church Morn and Eve. Mr and Mrs Wilson drank Tea with us, after Supper I sat an hour at Mrs Mawer's.

7 April 1765

One of Easter Sunday's two church services was probably Communion, which in Georgian times was celebrated only about four times a year.

Monday 8 Violent rain all day, in the Eve Wind and hail. Mama and I drank tea at Mr Wilson's. In the Eve Miss Mawer came in.

April 9 Excessive Cold day, wind and rain. Mr and Mrs Wilson drank Tea and spent the Evening with us. Mrs Mawer and Miss came in.

April 10 Extremely Cold, got all my ruf[f]les drawn. In the Morn Mrs Colingwood brought me two Slips of Bulm of Gillood. At 2 o'Clock a most violent storm of Wind hail and rain. In the Evening Mrs Mawer and Miss came in.

10 April 1765

The Diarist seems very proud of her skill making ruffles. The 'two slips of bulm of Gillood' is one of the most difficult phrases in the diary to interpret. The medicinal Balm of Gilead is one possibility, which might have provided a soothing aromatic concoction, either for herself or Mama, or possibly for Revd Emerson since she wrote to Winston the next day. A slip might have been a twist of waxed paper containing the cream.

Thursday 11 Rain and wind, very Cold. Writing to Winston. In the Eve Mama and I sat an hour at Mrs Mawer's.

Friday 12 Remarkable Cold, in the Garden half an hour. Mrs Medcalf Widow and Mr F. Allen drank Tea with us. After Supper Miss Mawer and Mrs Wilson came in for half an hour.

12 April 1765

Today's tea party extends beyond the usual group, including not only Francis Allen but also Eleanor Metcalfe, widow of a London doctor.

April 13 Extreamly Cold, Betty Beautyment drank tea with us. I paid the Miller for Corn 3L. 5s. 3d. I went in to se Mr Wilson, he is very lame with the rheumatism. After Supper I sat an hour at Mrs Mawer's. Rainey Night.

13 April 1765

Farmer Betty Beautyment is likely to have been selling her butter in Richmond's Saturday market, before taking herself to the Diarist's home for taking tea while she was in the town. The miller's bill was presumably for a quantity of corn, perhaps a year's supply. Mr Wilson's incapacity due to rheumatism suggests he was an elderly man.

Sunday 14 Fine day, but Cold, at Church Morn and Even. Mrs Newsum drank Tea with us, Miss Mawer in the Eve. I sent a letter by her to Winston, she goes to Gainford in the Morn.

Monday 15 Fine day, Mama and I drank Tea with Mrs Mawer. In the Garden an hour. Miss Mawer brought me a letter from Winston with a better account of my Uncle than in the last.

15 April 1765

Bridget Mawer was able to travel to, and return from, Gainford in one day. Her route evidently took her across the new bridge at Winston, close by the rectory. She was able to deliver a letter from the Diarist on the way there and bring an immediate reply back.

Tuesday 16 Fine day. Mrs Bosamworth call'd for half an hour. Old Mrs Hodgson buried, widow. Mrs Mawer and Miss drank Tea with us.

16 April 1765

The parish register records the burial of Elizabeth Hodgson widow. The Diarist's circle is largely made up of widows, and the demise of one of them is duly noted, presumably having been discussed during the day.

Wednesday 17 Cold rain all day, Mr and Mrs Wilson came in to tel us they had got a new Border from Newcastle, Miss Carr, Miss Mawer came in for me to join for half an hour.

17 April 1765

That we know where Miss Carr comes from marks her out as one of the few pupils at the Wilsons' school about whom we have this information. It is interesting that the recruiting distance has expanded as far away as Newcastle. This may explain why Mr Wilson seems often to have been away from Richmond during the week.

Thursday 18 Fine day but Cold, down Street at Mrs Dixon's, drank Tea at Mrs Newsum's along with Mrs Robinson and Miss and Mrs Medcalf. In the Eve Miss Mawer and Mrs Wilson came in.

Friday 19 Cold Showers of rain. Ironing in the Morn, in the Eve Miss Mawer came in. Mr and Mrs Wilson Suped with us, Rainey Night.

19 April 1765

The Wilsons are among the few friends who stay to eat with the Diarist.

Saturday 20 Rainey Morn, ironing. Mrs Mawer and Miss drank Tea with us, in the Eve the Revd. Mr Nichhols sat half an hour, he is going for Cambridge on Monday. A Child of Ralph Wadkins buried. Rainey Night.

20 April 1765

Revd Christopher Nicholls had visited the Diarist four times while back home in Richmond, so his company would doubtless be missed. After Sidney Sussex College, his first curacies were also in Cambridge. The child who died was Ralph Watkin's daughter Jane. His wife and two other daughters had also recently died.

Sunday 21 Extreamly Cold, at Church Morn and Eve. Mama and I drank Tea at Mr Wilson's. Old Mrs Heath buried. Rainey Night. Miss Mawer came in.

21 April 1765

St Mary's Parish Church must have been very cold for those two services, and for those attending the burial in the churchyard of widow Mary Heath.

Monday 22 Cold rain all day. Mrs Wilson came in.

April 23 a violent Storm last night of Thunder, Lightning, Hail and Rain, very badly all day. In the Evening Mr Wilson came in, and Mr Key Mawer and Miss and sat an hour.

23 April 1765

The Diarist's interest in the weather provides us with a detailed description of the storm. Revd Kay Mawer, at home from the Midlands, visited with his sister.

April 24 Cold with some showers, in the Eve Miss Mawer came in.

April 25 Mr Reuben Killburn Buried. In the Eve Mrs Wilson came to real [reel?] Miss Mawer came to bad[e] us farewell, she leaves the town tomorrow Morn.

25 April 1765

The cold weather seems to have resulted in even more funerals than usual. Reuben Kilburn had only recently remarried, his second wife being a relative of the Readheads. Mrs Wilson was probably reeling some spun yarn ready for knitting or weaving. Bridget Mawer's moving away will leave a hole in the Diarist's circle.

Friday 26 I got a letter from Miss Bell Emerson after dinner. Mrs Mawer came in for half an hour. Mr and Mrs Wilson drank Tea with us, Mrs Close gave us a call, they go to Easby to live tomorrow. John Thompson buried.

26 April 1765

John Close, a wealthy man of an important Richmond family, and his younger wife Elizabeth were moving with their young family of eight children to Easby House. For once it is not a widow whose burial is noted.

April 27 The Weather Cold with Showers. Mrs Mawer came in.

Sunday 28 Rain in the Morn, at Church Morn and Eve. Mrs Bowes drank Tea with us. After Tea I sat half an hour with Mrs Mawer and her son, he goes to York tomorrow. After Supper Mrs Wilson came in.

28 April 1765

The reference could be to either of Mrs Mawer's two sons. Revd John Mawer was a cleric in the Lincoln area, and Revd Kay Mawer in the Lichfield diocese, so either could have travelled through York, though we know that Kay had been in Richmond a few days earlier.

Monday 29 Fine day, in the Garden an hour. Mrs Wilson drank Tea with us. I sat an hour with Mrs Mawer.

April 30 Fine Morn, Mama and I at Prayers. Some Showers of rain in the Afternoon. I walk down to Mrs Dixon's Shop. In the Eve Mrs Mawer came in.

30 April 1765

The Diarist and her mother unusually attend church on a Tuesday.

May 1 Rain all day, Mama and I drank Tea at Mrs Mawer's. Mr Sewdale there. In the Eve Mrs Wilson came in, they have got a new Border, Miss Foss from Brough.

1 May 1765

Miss Foss was the daughter of William Foss, who lived on the Brough estate near Catterick.

May the 2 Extremely Cold, in the Eve Mrs Wilson came in. After Supper Mrs Mawer sat an hour with us.

Friday 3 Tolerable fine day, Mrs Wilson drank Tea with us. I had a walk with her and her Young Ladies. In the Eve Mrs Mawer and Mrs Wilson came in.

3 May 1765

The number of young women enrolled at the Wilsons' school is rising.

May 4 In the Morn Mr Allen call'd upon us, he got to town yesterday. Mrs Mawer drank Tea with us, in the Eve I went into Mr Wilson's. Miss York dead.

4 May 1765

It would seem that the conversation over tea or in the evening at Mr Wilson's had brought the sad news that Sophia Anne, the little daughter of John and Sophia Yorke, had died.

Sunday 5 Fine day, at Church in the Morn. After dinner I had a walk in Mr York's Garden with Mr and Mrs Medcalf. Mr and Mrs Newsam drank Tea at Mrs Newsam's. In the Eve Mrs Mawer and Mrs Readhead came in.

5 May 1765

The planned day for opening the grounds of Yorke House to visitors seems to have gone ahead despite the family's tragedy.

Monday 6 Wet morn, fine Afternoon. Mr and Mrs Mawer drank Tea with us.

Tuesday 7 Wet Morn. Mr Sewdale drank Tea with us. Miss Stricklands call'd upon me to walk, Mrs Mawer came in for half an hour, and Mrs Wilson.

7 May 1765

The mysterious Mr Sewdale is in the tea-drinking circle this week, gentlemen being only occasionally included. It would seem that Barbara Strickland has joined her sister Catherine in the promenading group.

Wednesday 8 Fine day, in the Garden two hours. Mr Allen call'd in for half an hour, in the Eve Mrs Mawer.

8 May 1765

William Allen, whose sister was married to the Diarist's brother, had arrived from London for a stay of some weeks. Based at the royal court, he regularly returned to his native Richmond, and always visited the Diarist as soon as he arrived in the town, probably to report news of her brother Layton. William called on the Diarist every few days while there, and saw her before he left.

Thursday 9 Fine day, in the Garden with Mama and Mrs Mawer. Mr and Mrs Wilson drank Tea with us, Mrs Mawer came in.

May the 10 in the Garden an hour. Mama and I drank Tea with Mrs Mawer, and Mr Sewdale. Mr Allen call'd, I wrote to my Uncle Smith, by Mama's order, and sent the Certificate. Miss York buried in a very private manner at 10 o'clock at night.

10 May 1765

William Allen's visit seems to have prompted the need to write to uncle Thomas Smith. The phrase 'by Mama's order' and the nature of the certificate are not yet understood. The burial of little Sophia Anne in the Yorke family vault in St Mary's parish church took place at what seems to us a strange hour, but at the time this was normal for gentry families. It would need a lot of candles to light the way down the awkward narrow staircase leading into the vault, carrying even a very small coffin. The 'private manner' here described was perhaps due to the extremely distraught state from which her mother never recovered.

Saturday 11 in the Morn I went in to se Miss Mawer, fine day. Mrs Mawer and Miss drank Tea with us and bad[e] us farewell, they are going to live at Gainford. Mr Allen call'd for half an hour.

11 May 1765

The move of Mrs and Miss Mawer to Gainford would mark a big change in the Diarist's routine as they had all spent so much time in each other's company. William Allen may have been checking up that his advice had been followed over what needed to be sent to London.

Sunday 12 Fine day, very indifferent all day. Mrs Panton drank Tea with us, Mr & Mrs Wilson in the Eve.

Monday 13 very fine day, in the Garden half an hour. Mrs Wilson and I had a walk to Love lane to drink Tea with E. Beatiment, she is lately marry'd.

13 May 1765

Elspeth (Eppey to the Diarist) was the only daughter in Betty and Joseph Beautyment's family of five and was now just 21.

Tuesday 14 fine day, I was down Street at the Shops, got Mama a Poplin Gown at 2s. 1d. a yard. My Sister got a letter from Betty Nichols, Mr and Mrs Wilson came in in the Even.

The spell of fine early Spring weather has prompted the Diarist to do some shopping. She regularly buys clothes for her Mama when she is doing the rounds of the Richmond shops. Betty was the youngest of the Nicholls family.

May the 15 I got a letter from Winston, with an ac[c]ount of poor Mr Tidy's Death and some flower seeds which I have been set[t]ing. Finish'd my Ruffles. Mr and Mrs Wilson drank Tea with us.

15 May 1765

The demise of 'poor Mr Tidy' was obviously important enough for one of the Emersons to write to inform the Diarist of it. He was John Tidy of Staindrop, the father of Revd Thomas Holmes Tidy, Revd Emerson's curate at Great Stainton, and later rector of Redmarshal. Creating ruffles, the elaborate frills applied round the edge of a dressy apron, took a lot of meticulous work.

May 16 Thos Medcalf in the Garden, Mama and I drank Tea at Mr Wilson's. Fine Weather.

Friday 17 Thos in the Garden. Mrs Medcalf, Mrs Newsam and Miss Hog drank Tea with us, we had a walk in the Evening.

17 May 1765

Thomas Metcalfe the gardener is most likely completely unrelated to the Diarist's friends the Metcalfes, but Miss Hogg was probably a relative of Mrs Metcalfe, formerly Jane Hogg.

May 18 Mrs Readhead and Mrs Wilson drank Tea with us.

Sunday 19 very indifferent, not at Church. Miss Turnbull and Mrs F. Dixon drank Tea with us. We had a letter from Minny Smith, and a Note from Miss Mawer. Mr and Mrs Wilson in the Eve.

19 May 1765

Minny Smith was the Diarist's niece Wilhelmina who lived in London. The postboy seems to have brought two communications that Sunday, as Bridget Mawer too had sent some account of her new life in Gainford.

Monday 20 Mrs F. Dixon and I walk'd to Easby to make a visit for Mrs Close.

20 May 1765

John and Elizabeth Close and their many children, a well-to-do family who were probably good customers of Faith Dixon's drapery shop, had recently moved to Easby House, a large property belonging to the Smith family.

May 21 down Street at the Shops. Drank Tea with Mrs Newsam. In the Eve Mr & Mrs Wilson & Mrs Readhead.

May 22 In the Garden half an hour. Writeing to Miss Bell Emerson. In the Eve a Shower of Rain.

22 May 1765

The letter to Isabel Emerson is probably to update that branch of the family on the news sent from London by niece Minny. However, it seems not to get posted until the Saturday.

May 23 very Cold with Showers of rain and hail, after Tea down Street at Mrs Dixon's. Mrs Wilson and Mrs Readhead came in.

Friday 24 Extreamly Cold, Violent Shower of hail. Mr Wilson has got a new border, Miss Dickinson [of] Scorton. Dr Pringle and Mr Wilson drank Tea with us.

24 May 1765

The Wilsons' new boarder Miss Dickinson was the daughter of Revd Timothy Dickonson[sic], vicar of Grinton and also Perpetual Curate of Bolton-on-Swale. Grinton then having no vicarage, he had built a house for his curate near Grinton bridge in 1762. Bolton also had no parsonage, but the incumbent usually lived at Scorton, often in the grammar school there. Men were better represented at this day's tea drinking session than was usual.

Saturday 25 Cold as ever, got a letter from Miss Jenney Emerson, sent my letter to Winston. Miss Mawer came to Town and dined with us. I went down to the Shops with her, and we drank Tea at Mrs Chapman's. In the Eve Mrs Readhead came in.

25 May 1765

Jenny Emerson was doubtless writing to tell the Diarist about her forthcoming marriage. Bridget Mawer, visiting from Gainford, was included in the family dinner, which was followed by an afternoon shopping expedition. Girls traditionally wore new clothes on Whit Sunday up until World War I.

Whit Sunday 26 at Church morn and Eve. Extreamly Cold with rain and hail. Mr and Mrs Wilson drank Tea with us, in the Eve I sat half an hour with Mrs Simpson.

26 May 1765

Whit Sunday was then treated as a holiday, a rare opportunity for leisure and relaxation, so it must have been disappointing that the weather was not more favourable.

Monday the 27 very Cold, the Militia comeing in to stay a Month. A Company of Players are come to Town, this is the first Night of their performing, the Play is the Constant Couple, or a Trip to the Jubilee, with Damon & Phillida. Mr Allen was so kind as sending my Sister and I Tickets, and Miss Carr to go with us. My sister sent her Ticket to Mrs Wilson, Mr F. Allen drank Tea with us.

27 May 1765

The actors arrived to coincide with the Militia muster. The London-based William Allen would be familiar with theatrical fashions there, and to encourage his somewhat impoverished Richmond in-laws to attend the plays, he treated them to tickets. They could show the Wilsons' scholar Miss Carr how to behave at a theatrical performance. However, the Diarist's sister typically chose not to go to such a social event.

May the 28 very Cold, Mama and I drank Tea at Mr Wilson's. Mr Allen call'd, he goes for London in the Morn. Mama sent her two grandaughters each of them half a Crown by Mr Allen.

28 May 1765

William Allen was used as a courier to take some money to Anne and Wilhelmina Smith in London.

May the 29 Cold weather. We had Betty Taylor and her little girl in the afternoon, in the Eve I walk'd down to Mrs Newsam's.

May 30 In the Eve I went down to Mrs Newsam's to ask her to walk but it was so Cold we did not go.

30 May 1765

It was no wonder that the heavily pregnant Mrs Newsham did not feel like a walk on a cold evening, but she was able to enjoy a crowded visit to the play 'Richard III' the following evening.

Friday 31 Mama and I drank Tea with Mrs Wilson. I went with Mrs Medcalf and Mrs Newsam to the Play to Richard the third, a full house.

June 1 very Cold. Writeing to Winston, my Sister got a letter from Miss Pye, one inclos'd for Miss Mawer with some patterns, Betty Beautiment and her Daughter drank Tea with us.

1 June 1765

Miss Pye, the friend in Dr Pringle's circle, who has moved away from Richmond, seemingly has not heard that Bridget Mawer has moved to Gainford. It would be interesting to know more about the patterns, perhaps samples of dress materials newly fashionable in London.

June 2 at Church Morn and Eve, Mrs Colingham and Mrs Mayson drank Tea with us, Mr and Mrs Wilson spent the Evening.

2 June 1765

Other ladies appear in the Tea group, perhaps to fill the gap left by the departure of Hannah and Bridget Mawer.

Visitation Monday 3 at Church, Mr Peacock preach'd. Mr Moor drank Tea with us. Mrs Wilson & I had a walk, very Cold.

3 June 1765

The Visitation, either by the Bishop of Chester or the Archdeacon of Richmond, was an important event for a parish church, and visitation sermons were often published. No other preachers are mentioned in the diary. It is likely that the Diarist knew John Peacock as one of her clerical uncle's curates. Revd Moore had presumably also been at the service.

June 4 I walk'd down Street, drank Tea at Mrs Newsam's, in the Morn at Mrs Simpson's to see the Men fire. Got a letter from C. Jenny Emerson to inform us that my Aunt and she wou'd be here on Thursday to spend the day with us.

4 June 1765

> *As cousin Jane Emerson was getting married exactly a week later, it seems surprising that she and her mother would have time to break off from wedding preparations to spend a day with the Diarist's family in Richmond. It doesn't sound as though last minute shopping was planned, so perhaps there were other important matters to discuss.*

June 5 Tolerable fine day. Mama & I drank Tea at Mr Wilson's.

Thursday 6 greatly disappointed in not seeing our friends according to appointment. Mr and Mrs Wilson drank Tea.

6 June 1765

> *It is understandable that the Diarist would be so disappointed that her aunt and cousin had cancelled the pre-wedding visit. Something (unexplained in the Diary) seems to have happened somewhere in the family, for the Diarist did not in the end attend her cousin's wedding.*

Friday 7 Mama very badly, we sat in her room all day.

June 8 Fine day. Cousn Jenny Emerson came alone to spend the day with us. We were down Street at the Shops. I got a new hatt 4s. 5d.

8 June 1765

> *How did Jenny manage to make her solo visit so near to the wedding? Or did she need some last-minute clothes shopping that market day? Was the Diarist's new hat intended for the wedding? Let us hope it came in for some other event, because she did not go to the wedding.*

Sunday 9 Very hot day, at Church Morn and Eve, a shower of rain in the afternoon. Arranged a visit to Mrs Strickland, in the Eve Mr & Mrs Wilson.

Monday 10 hot day, Mrs Bosamworth spent the day with us. In the Eve I went to Mrs Dixon's.

June 11 in the Garden an hour, Mr and Mrs Wilson drank Tea and spent the Eve. This day Miss Jenny Emerson was marry'd at Winston to Mr Headlam of Newcastle. Ant'y Dixon's son buried.

11 June 1765

> *An hour in the garden can hardly have compensated for not attending her cousin's wedding. Revd Emerson's curate from his other parish of Great Stainton, Thomas Holmes Tidy, performed the ceremony at Winston Church for Jane Emmerson's marriage to Thomas Emerson Headlam of Gateshead, presumably a distant relation. The Diarist knew Anthony Dixon well, for he originated from Winston, he and his wife Anne had a large family.*

June the 12 Very unpleasant day, wind and Showers of rain. Mama and I drank Tea at Mr Wilson's.

June the 13 After Tea I went to Mr Simpson and got my self a black Shalon Petticoat at 1s. 9d. a yd. Call'd at Matty's. Sat half an hour at Mrs Newsam's.

13 June 1765

> *The superior draper's shop of mercer Thomas Simpson sold the relatively expensive fine wool material to make a black petticoat, a type of skirt to show under a split gown.*

Friday 14 A fine rain all day, my Sister wrote to Matthew Graham in Ireland. In the Eve Mr and Mrs Wilson. William Hodgson's Wife buried.

14 June 1765

> *The family's link with Matthew Graham is unclear, but his name occurs several times in the diary. The correspondence with him is of a business nature. William Hodgson, whose wife Elizabeth had died, was a Richmond carrier, and perhaps had often taken the Diarist or the Emersons to and from Winston.*

Saturday 15 My Sister got a letter from Co[usi]n F. Emerson with some of Mrs Headlam's Bride Cake. My Sister wrote to Miss Mawer, with some patterns and a letter from Miss Pye. Showers of rain.

15 June 1765

At least they got a taste of Jane Emerson's wedding cake! It had taken the Diarist's tardy sister two weeks to forward Miss Pye's patterns to Bridget Mawer!

Sunday 16 At Church Morn & Eve, Mr and Mrs Wilson spent the Eve with us. Shower of rain.

Monday 17 In the Garden an hour, fine, Showers of rain.

June 18 My Sister got a letter from Miss F. Emerson, one inclos'd from Minny Smith. Miss Emerson got to Winston from London last Saturday. Mr George Hutchinson and his wife and Matty Beauley drank Tea with us. Mrs Medcalf and Miss Pencop gave us a call. Mrs Wilson supd with us, Mrs Readhead came in.

18 June 1765

Fanny Emerson seems to have been the scribe in the Emerson family, just as the Diarist's sister was in hers. The eldest Winston cousin, Elizabeth, had brought from London a letter from the Diarist's niece Wilhelmina, containing family news.

June 19 dull day but no rain, Mr & Mrs Wilson drunk Tea.

Thursday 20 I drank Tea at Mrs Medcalf's. We had a walk with Mr and Mrs Newsam.

20 June 1765

The indomitable Betty Newsam is within a few days of giving birth to her son William.

Friday 21 in the Garden half an hour. Miss Strickland call'd to ask me to go to the play, her Mama has orderd one tonight; I did not go.

21 June 1765

Catherine Strickland, the mother, had long been a follower of drama in Richmond. Her account book provides our first reference, in 1755, to Georgian players visiting the town. Here she had 'ordered' a play for her daughters. Perhaps the Diarist could not afford a ticket.

Saturday 22 My Sister got a letter from Miss Mawer, Betty Beautiment drank Tea. Down Street in the Eve.

June 23 at Church Morn and Eve, the day windey with some showers of rain. I drank Tea with Miss Turnbull. In the Eve Mr and Mrs Wilson came in.

Monday 24 I maid a visit to Mrs Panton, call'd upon Mrs Simpson, she was deliver'd of a Girl last night. Disagreeable wind. Mr F. Allen drank tea with Mama. Mrs Bosamworth call'd.

24 June 1765

The Mawers' friend Mrs Panton would be interested to hear the news recently received from Bridget. New baby Mary was the daughter of Thomas Simpson, the mercer, who sold elegant dress fabrics.

June 25 In the Morn Miss Carr and I walk'd to Love lane. The two Mrs Colingwood's drank Tea with us. At 7 o'clock I went to the Town's Hall to hear Mr McGeorge's lecture upon Heads.

25 June 1765

The Wilsons' pupil Miss Carr joined the Diarist in a walk to the farmhouse of her friend Betty Beautyment. The actor and musician Horatio Thomas McGeorge had brought a group of players to the town for a series of summer performances. His avant-garde 'Lecture upon Heads' was a daringly satirical one-man presentation, incorporating model heads, originally devised in London only the previous year, and subsequently widely copied by other actors, as here in Richmond, one of its earliest performances in the north of England.

June the 26 Cold rain great part of the day, Mr and Mrs Wilson drank tea with us.

Thursday 27 in the Garden half an hour. At 5 o'clock I went to Robert Boweses Funeral. In the Eve A. Nickhols call'd, she is thust comd from London.

27 June 1765

One of the Diarist's typical days – news from the capital via her friend Alice Nichols after a local funeral, in this case of soldier Robert Bowes who had married Sally, the daughter of her landlords the Readheads. He left behind two small children.

Friday 28 in the Eve Mr and Mrs Wilson came in.

June 29 fine day, in the Eve down Street at Mrs Newsam's.

29 June 1765

The visit to the Newsams was probably to see their new baby boy, William.

Sunday 30 Betty Beautement's son carry'd me to Winston. We got there to Church in the Morn, in the afternoon cousin Fanny and I made a Visit to Mrs Mawer and Miss at Gainford.

30 June 1765

An example of how much travel the Diarist could achieve. The son of her farmer friend Betty Beautyment would have access to a cart, and could get her from Richmond to Winston in time for morning worship at the church there. Possibly her uncle, Revd John Emerson, had sufficiently recovered from his illness to take the service. The Emerson family probably had a chaise or similar transport which enabled Fanny and the Diarist to see how Hannah and Bridget Mawer were getting on in their new life at Gainford.

July the 1 After dinner I set forward to Richmond, got home to Tea. At 8 o'clock went to the play, the Conscious Lovers.

1 July 1765

A busy day with the journey back from Winston, followed by an evening out at the play, interestingly performed on a Monday evening. This time the Diarist can afford a ticket; perhaps the Emersons had given her some money.

July 2 hot day, in the Garden in the morning.

Wednesday 3 July In the Garden puling Strawberrys. In the Eve I went to se Mrs Newsam, she got a son Easter Monday morn.

3 July 1765

The Diarist's friend, Betty Newsham, had almost certainly given birth to her baby William much more recently than

Easter Monday (8 April that year). He was baptised in Richmond parish church on 1 July, baptisms then usually taking place when the infant was just a few days old. Even Whit Monday would have been in late May. Was this a rare mistake by the Diarist?

Thursday 4 Mr and Mrs Wilson drank Tea with us.

Friday 5 in the Morn puling strawberrys, after dinner I went to se Mrs Newsam and Mrs Simpson, got home to Tea. Mrs Chapman came and sat an hour.

5 July 1765

The prolific crop of strawberries that summer enabled the Diarist to share them with many of her friends, presumably including both these mothers of new babies.

Fair Day 6 in the Eve I went to Mrs Dixon's shop. Mrs Wilson and her Sister Mrs Croft came in and sat an hour. A Shower of rain. An Old Man buried.

6 July 1765

This Saturday was not only market day but also the day of the Rake Fair, one of Richmond's ancient chartered fairs. It was held on the Saturday before the feast of the reburial of the remains of St Thomas Becket into his shrine in Canterbury Cathedral (7 July). Ann Wilson's elder sister, Hannah Croft, was visiting from York. The burial was of Edward Branson, a stonemason who would be well known in the town.

Sunday 7 Windy, dull day, at Church Morn and Eve. I made a visit to Mrs Medcalf and her n[e]ice. Miss Mawer came home with me from Church and sat half an hour, she is at the Green. Mrs Nichols and her daughter Alice drank Tea with Mama and Sister.

7 July 1765

Bridget Mawer was staying with the Yorke family at Yorke House on The Green. Had she sat in their family gallery up on the south side of the chancel for the church service? Many former residents seem to have returned to Richmond in order to enjoy the excitement of the Rake Fair, including Alice Nicholls.

Monday 8 in the Morn puling Strawberrys, sent a plate to Mrs Wilson. After Tea I went to Mrs Dixon's, call'd at Mrs Newsam's.

8 July 1765

Faith Dixon's and James Newsam's shops were next door to one another on the High Row of the Market Place, so it was easy to visit both households.

July 9 Rain the greatest part of the [day]. Mr and Mrs Wilson and her two Sisters, Mrs Row and Mrs Croft and her aunt Mrs Barker drank Tea with us.

9 July 1765

There is a large gathering of the Johnson family, not only Ann Wilson but also Mary Raw from Richmond and Hannah Croft from York, plus their aunt.

July 10 in the Garden puling Strawberrys, sent a plaite to Mrs Colingwood. I went to the Play with Mrs Newsam and Miss Mewbank to se the Miser and the Mayor of Garret. A Child buried.

10 July 1765

The three ladies went together to the plays, apparently without any menfolk, seeing Fielding's old favourite and Foote's recent farce.

July 11 puling Strawberry's, sent some to Matty's and Mr. F. Allen. Mama & I drank Tea at Mrs Wilson's. They came with us and got some Strawberrys.

Friday 12 badly all day, se nobody.

12 July 1765

Perhaps there had been a surfeit of strawberries? It was a brief indisposition, for the Diarist was able to socialise the following evening.

July the 13 down Street in the Eve at Mrs Dixon's and Mrs Newsam's.

Sunday 14 very hot day, at Church Morn and Eve. After Tea Mr and Mrs Wilson and I had a walk.

Monday 15 Puling Strawberrys, sent some to Matty. She sent me Ticket for the Play, Mr McGeorge's Benefit, Venice Preserv'd, the Farce the Citizen.

15 July 1765

Licensee of the 'King's Arms Inn', Matty Beauly, may have acted as the 'box office' for the players, and perhaps showed her appreciation for the Diarist's strawberries by sending her a free ticket. That Horatio Thomas McGeorge had a benefit night indicates that he was the leader of that particular company of players.

July 16 Puling Strawberrys. Miss Carr and Miss Close from Mrs Wilson's drank Tea with us & A. Nichols. The young Ladies got Strawberrys and Cream. Dr Pringle call'd.

16 July 1765

It is interesting that in 1765 not only were strawberries and cream already being served together, but were considered a treat to be shared with the pupils of the Wilsons' school.

July 17 Mr and Mrs Wilson drank Tea with us.

July 18 Puling Strawberrys. Mama and I walk'd into the Paddock. Mr & Mrs Wilson supped with us upon Strawberrys.

18 July 1765

The Paddock was not far from Bowes Hall, being just east of what were then the limits of St Mary's Churchyard. However it would require Mama to negotiate a steep downhill and uphill return.

July 19 in the Garden weeding. After dinner Mrs Hutchinson came in with her little boy for half an hour. Paid Mrs Readhead the half year's rent due Mayday 5L. 0s. 0d. My Sister got a letter from Cousin Fanny Emerson by Solomon Blades.

19 July 1765

In 1760 Richmond girl Mary Binks had married George Hutchinson, a soldier in the Durham Militia. He later worked as an agent for the Earl of Holderness and Sir Lawrence Dundas. In Kirkby Ravensworth churchyard there is a tombstone commemorating Hutchinson and his son, also George. This little

*boy, who visited the Diarist with his mother, attended Richmond
Grammar School and went up to Trinity College, Cambridge,
where he became a Fellow. The Diarist was obviously very late
paying her half year's rent of £5 due at May Day, which was
probably the anniversary of when she had moved to Richmond.
Richmond shoemaker Solomon Blades had seemingly travelled
into Teesdale and acted as courier for Fanny Emerson's letter. This
perhaps warned the Diarist that Fanny's mother and elder sister
were on their way to Richmond.*

July 20 Puling Strawberrys. After dinner down Street at several
places, drank Tea at Mrs Newsam's.

Sunday 21 at Church Morn & Eve, disagreeable wind. Thust as
we were set down to Tea came my Aunt and Miss Emerson, they
stay'd all night.

21 July 1765

*Wherever Ann and Elizabeth Emerson had travelled from, it
would seem they could not get as far as Winston that evening.*

July 22 Fine Showers of rain. After breakfast the Ladies went home.

July 23 After Tea I went down to Mrs Newsam's. Mr George
Thompson Buried.

23 July 1765

*George Thompson was a mercer and tailor. The title 'Mr', afforded
by both the Diarist and the parish register, shows he had a
status in the town, and in fact was a member of the corporation's
Common Council and took his turn at various civic duties.*

July 24 I made a Visit to Mrs Pringle, from thence we went to a
Concert at the Town's Hall. We Subscribed 1s. 6d. for one night.

24 July 1765

*A rare indication of the Diarist providing us with the cost of
Richmond's social events. The concert may have been provided by
the players who were musicians as well as actors.*

July 25 Mr Wayne bled Mama. Starching and drying Small Cloths.
Mrs Layton Buried.

25 July 1765

There is no indication that Mama has recently been unwell, so Dr Wayne's bleeding her was presumably a routine task. The small cloths so carefully attended to as being worth mentioning in the diary were probably connected with tea drinking.

Friday 26 Ironing in the Morn, in the Eve Mr Allen call'd. He got to Town last night from London.

26 July 1765

This entry is an excellent example of how Richmond people were kept in close touch with what was happening in London.

July 27 Ironing in the Morn. After dinner Mr Moor call'd for half an hour. In the Eve Miss Mawbeck and I had a walk.

27 July 1765

Revd Moore from Teesdale has called again; doubtless the Diarist's family enjoyed hearing news from those parts.

Sunday 28 Extreamly hot, at Church Morn & Eve. Mrs Chapman drank Tea with us.

July 29 Ironing in the Morn, Mr and Mrs Close drank Tea with us. I went down to se Hannah Cowling, she is lyeing in of her 16th Child. Two Funerals Harry Wilson & Hannah Cowling's Child.

29 July 1765

Hannah Cowling was the wife of John Cowling, one of Richmond's many blacksmiths. Her sixteenth child, Moses, had only been baptised on 27 July. Hannah would not have been able to attend the infant's funeral.

July 30 Finish'd my Ironing, extream hot day, I got a letter from Cousin F. Emerson.

July 31 Excessive hot day. After dinner I went to se Matty, she has been Ill but is better. Alice Nichols call'd and supped with us.

31 July 1765

Poor Matty Beauly was unfortunately not much better as she would shortly be diagnosed with jaundice. Alice Nicholls has not yet returned to London.

August 1 Extreamly hot. After dinner I went to Mrs Dixon's, and go[t] a yard of Irish Cloth 4s. 5d. yd, drank Tea with Mrs Newsam. Ann Cooper buried.

1 August 1765

The single yard of Irish cloth was very expensive at 4s. 5d. a yard. Perhaps it was a special type of linen lace? The parish register records the burial of 'Anne Cowper', presumably pronounced Cooper as the Diarist has noted it.

Friday 2 Mama and I at prayers in the Morn. I drank Tea with Matty. Extreamly hot.

2 August 1765

The Diarist and her mother have again attended the Friday version of Morning Prayer. Poor Matty Beauly's return to taking Tea was to be short-lived.

August 3 A Shower of rain, in the Eve, I went to se Matty, she has got the jaundice.

Sunday 4 Mama and I at Church, and after Church I sat an hour with Matty, in the Eve I had a walk with Mrs Medcalf and Miss Mawbank. Old Mrs Wycliffe dead at Harragate.

4 August 1765

Old Mrs Wycliffe, perhaps suffering from rheumatics, had probably gone to take the sulphur waters at Harrogate, which was becoming a fashionable spa town. Its season began in late July, so she may not have been there long when she died.

Monday 5 fine Showers of rain. After Tea Mrs Chapman sat half an hour. After Supper Mr and Mrs Wilson.

Tuesday 6 Recevd a letter from Nanny Smith by Mr Allen.

Another letter from the Diarist's sister-in-law has arrived from London without the cost of postage.

Wednesday 7 In the Garden an hour, Mrs Medcalfe, Mrs Newsam and Miss Mawbank drank Tea with us. A Poor Woman Buried. In the Eve Mrs Wilson came in, Mr Sewdale call'd for half an hour.

Miss Mawbank seems to be a friend of Mrs Medcalf and so was probably a young woman. The Diarist had a lot of company in one day. The reference to the burial of Mary, the wife of Leonard Metcalfe, may indicate that the cost had to be borne by the parish poor law system.

Thursday 8 dull day, Mrs Strickland and Miss Charlotte call'd, after Tea I walk'd down Street.

Friday 9 Mama got a bad Cold. Mr Jackson came to take measure of me for a pair of Stays. Mrs Wilson brought Mama two moorcocks.

Stays were a vital piece of Georgian underclothing, and the several staymakers working in the town were important craftsmen. The Diarist would pay Robert Jackson £1 5s for his handiwork. Mama seems to have been very partial to moorcock, as she had been given one by Kay Mawer early the previous August. The tradition of not opening the shooting season before 12 August had not yet been enshrined in law.

August 10 a shower of rain. Mrs Moor, Miss Moor, the Captain and Master Tommy drank Tea with us.

Sunday 11 At Church in the Morn. After Dinner I had a walk to Aske with Mr and Mrs Medcalf, Mr and Mrs Newsam, Miss Mawbank & Miss Hogg, we all drank Tea at Mr Medcalf's.

The party of seven that walked to Aske that Sunday afternoon formed a larger group than was usual for such of the Diarist's outings.

Augt 12 Mama badly in a Cold, sat in her own room. I went to se Hannah Cowling, Dr Pringle's servant came to invite me to Miss Hall's Funeral to be a bearer, we had White Hoods, Scarfes and Gloves. A fine Shower of rain.

<u>*12 August 1765*</u>

The solicitous Diarist pays a sympathetic visit to Hannah Cowling whose sixteenth child had recently died in infancy. Miss Hall was from Edinburgh, so her family, if she had any, would not be able to attend her burial. The kindly Dr Pringle, who had probably attended her in her final illness, sought the Diarist's support to act the following day as a chief mourner, rather than to carry the coffin as in the modern usage of the word bearer. The white mourning habit may have been in recognition of the lady's unmarried status.

Augt 13 Rain all the Morn, Mr Wayne came in. At 3 o'clock I went to the funeral. We got home without rain, in the Eve Mrs Wilson came in to se Mama. A young Man buried, he was brought from Northallerton, his name Hayward.

<u>*13 August 1765*</u>

Dr Wayne had come to visit Mama, who had a very bad cold. The parish church saw a second funeral this day. John Hayward, who was very unusually brought from Northallerton for burial in Richmond, was probably a member of a Richmond family, several of whom were surgeons and apothecaries.

Augt 14 In the Garden an hour, Cold Wind. Mr and Mrs Wilson drank Tea with us. Mrs Hutchinson at the Hall Buried at Cat[teric]k. In the Eve I had Miss Carr and Miss Hogg in the Garden to eat Goosbeers.

<u>*14 August 1765*</u>

Martha Hutchinson was of 'The Hill', or Hill House, a fine old house which looks down Frenchgate onto Richmond. She was the grandmother of Frances I'Anson, 'The Lass of Richmond Hill', although did not live to see her daughter Martha give birth to Frances in 1766. It sounds as though the gooseberries were a dessert variety which could be eaten raw in the garden.

Augt 15 Mama something better, not got down stairs yet. After Tea I went with Mr and Mrs Wilson to the Dancing School to se the Children dance. The Master came 3 week ago, his name Nichol. Peggy Close buried, she dyed in Childbed.

15 August 1765

This was probably the first time a Dancing Master had arrived in Richmond to teach children to dance. It was a seasonal job so they tended not to stay long, but several others are recorded later. The parish register records the burial of Henry Close's wife Margaret and daughter Martha, who had been baptised the previous day. Henry Close was one of a long line of Richmond butchers, and the Diarist was presumably one of his customers.

Friday 16 Fine Morn, in the Garden, after dinner I went down Street, call'd at Mrs Dixon's, drank Tea at Hannah Cowling's. Shower of rain.

16 August 1765

Hannah Cowling is up and about after her sad 'lying-in'.

Augt 17 Cold Air, walk'd down Street, went to bed very Ill.

17 August 1765

This is the start of the Diarist's prolonged bout of severe illness, which lasted until the end of the month. She took to her bed and only struggled to get up so her bed could be made. Dr Pringle paid her several visits. Mama was ill herself with a bad back, so it was Mrs Wilson who came in to sit with the two of them.

Sunday 18 very bad all day. Mrs Newsam and Mawbank call'd into the Garden to get Goosbeers, fine day.

18 August 1765

The garden is now producing a generous crop of gooseberries.

Monday 19 Extream ill, Violent pain in my Head and Stomach. In the Eve Mrs Wilson sat an hour with us.

Tuesday 20 Very bad, Mama Ill in the pain in her Back, hot day. Mrs Wilson sat the Eve with us.

The household must really be struggling with both Mama and the Diarist so poorly, seemingly with unrelated illnesses.

Augt 21 very badly, Mr & Mrs Wilson drank Tea with us.

Thursday 22 very Ill, in the Eve Mrs Wilson came in.

Friday 23 Extreamly Ill, sent for Dr. Pringle.

Augt 24 A great deal worse, obliged to go to bed, in the afternoon the Dr came to se me.

Sunday 25 I had a very bad night, got no sleep, in the Morn the Dr came to se me, in the Eve Mrs Wilson. Violent Thunder lightning, and rain in the Night.

Monday 26 very Ill, in the Eve Mrs Wilson came in.

Tuesday 27 very Ill, got up to have my bed made.

Augt 28 I sat up two hours, the Dr came to se me, my Sister sent a letter to Winston.

28 August 1765

It is likely that the letter to Winston was to tell the Emerson family of the poor health of both Mama and the Diarist.

Thursday 29 Something better, sat up half the day. Miss Close marryd to Mr Hilton.

29 August 1765

Anne Close, the 22-year-old daughter of Ralph Close, the town clerk of Richmond until his death in 1754, was the sister of John Close who had recently moved to Easby. Her new husband was Abraham Hilton of Hilton in County Durham, northwest of Darlington. Late in 1766 the couple would benefit financially from a complex sale of various properties in Richmond which had belonged to her two sisters as heiresses, not only of their father, but also his brother James who had no children. The properties included several tenanted by the Diarist's friends – Mrs Strickland in Newbiggin, George Hutchinson in Millgate and the blacksmith John Cowling. Thomas Cornforth, George Hutchinson and Christopher Wayne also benefited from the transaction, which saw the burgage rights of the properties sold to Sir Lawrence Dundas.

Friday 30 not so well as yesterday, got up at one o'clock, in the Eve Betty Nichols call'd to se me. Shower of rain. Two Funerals William Alderson and a Child.

30 August 1765

The young Betty Nicholls was a visitor who, we must hope, was a cheering presence after the long period of illness. The Diarist's improving health also means that she can again take an interest in the burials taking place at the parish church.

Saturday 31 better, we got a letter from Winston, my Sister sent an answer. Rain all day.

31 August 1765

The letter, rather than commiserating with Mama's and the Diarist's health problems, was probably to announce that Elizabeth and Fanny Emerson were arriving to stay for the race week. Sister's reply was obviously in the affirmative. The Diarist was still too weak to attend any of the social events until later in the race week.

Sepr 1 better, the Dr came to se me. In the Eve Miss Emerson and Miss Fanny came to stay the Race Week with us. In the Eve A. Nichols came in.

1 September 1765

Dr Pringle was likely making sure the Diarist's convalescence continued despite the houseguests. Alice Nicholls was probably a steadier companion than the carefree Emerson cousins.

Monday 2 fine morn, Miss Emerson walk'd down Street.

2 September 1765

The Diarist was too ill to accompany her cousin to the shops.

Sept 3 The first Race day, Mr Cornforth Horse won the 50L. Miss Emersons at the Assemble. I got down stayrs to dinner. In the morn Miss Jenny Cornforth call'd.

3 September 1765

William Cornforth, owner of the winning horse, was the brother of Thomas, the young Mayor of Richmond that year, with whom

Jane, known familiarly as Jenny, was probably staying for the races. She lived near Gainford, so would also know Bridget Mawer. The poor Diarist only managed to get downstairs to eat her dinner, while the cousins attended the evening assembly.

Sept 4 Mr Fenwick's Horse got the 50L. Rainey morning. Mr Mand call'd upon Miss Emerson. Miss Emerson at the Assemble, Miss Fanny danced.

Sept 5 Mr Fenwick's Horse got the Cup, and Mr Shaftoe's got the Sweepstakes. Miss Emersons and I were upon the Moor, fine day. Miss Emersons at the Assemble, both danced.

<u>5 September 1765</u>

At last the Diarist is well enough to get some fresh air on the new racecourse, presumably having had a ride up there. At least she has been kept up-to-date with the results of the most important horse races each day.

Friday 6 fine Morn, Miss Mawer call'd upon us, and two Miss Cornforths. In the Eve Miss Emerson partner call'd upon her, Cap[tai]n —. Miss Stricklands came in for half an hour, in the Eve Mr Allen came in.

<u>6 September 1765</u>

Let us hope all the visitors were not too tiring. Elizabeth Emerson seems to have been enjoying the attention of several suitors, though sadly she died early the following year without having married.

Saturday 7 fine day, Miss Emersons down Street. Cap[tai]n B. came in. Miss Emersons, Mama and my Self drank Tea at Mr Wilson's.

<u>7 September 1765</u>

The last day for the Emerson cousins to go down to the shops this market day, before returning home.

Sunday 8 fine day, Miss Emersons and I at Church in the Morn. Cap[tai]n B. drank Tea with us. After tea Miss Emersons went home.

<u>8 September 1765</u>

Elizabeth and Fanny Emerson had stayed a whole week, attending church in Richmond before returning home.

Monday 9 Fine day, in the Morn Mr Hill call'd upon us. Mr and Mrs Wilson drank tea with us. Mr Allen sat an hour.

Tuesday 10 Fine day I walk'd into the Garden, my Sister got a letter from Miss F. Emerson, one inclosd from Matthew Graham. In the Eve Mrs Wilson.

10 September 1765

At last the Diarist can enjoy a stroll in the garden. Matthew Graham's reply from Ireland seems to have come via Winston.

Sept 11 fine day, walk'd into the Garden. Dr Pringle drank tea with us.

Thursday 12 fine day, I went with Mrs Wilson to the dancing School. Mr and Mrs Wilson drank tea with us.

12 September 1765

The dancing school performances always seem to be on a Thursday.

Friday 13 fine day. Mr Nichols two Daughters and their Cousin Miss Lowes drank tea with us. At prayers in the Morn. Miss Peacup call'd, she goes home tomorrow.

13 September 1765

The lovely spell of September weather continues. A rare visit from Henry, the head of the Nicholls family, with his daughters Alice and Betty, and their cousin.

Sepr 14 fine day, I walk'd down Street, came home to tea.

14 September 1765

It sounds as though the visit to the shops on market day and on a fine day did not lead to the opportunity to have tea out.

Sunday 15 Shower of rain in the Morn, the rest of the day very pleasant, at Church in the Morn. After dinner I walk'd to Lovelane with Mr & Mrs Medcalf, Mr and Mrs Newsam and Miss Thompson, and drank tea there. A Child buried.

15 September 1765

It being a Sunday afternoon, two husbands can join the pleasant walk from Easby to the Beautyments' farmhouse for tea. It being a

Sunday did not prevent the churchyard being used for the burial of shoemaker George Lambert's son George.

Monday 16 A dull Cloudy day. At 11 o'clock a Hearse and two Post Chaises went past with Miss Pinkney to Darlington whear she is to be buried. Mama and I drank tea at Mr George Hutchinson's, Matty Beauly there. In the Eve Mrs Wilson came in and Suped with us. Mr Allen sat half an hour.

16 September 1765

An interesting description of an elaborate funeral cortège, with a hearse carrying the coffin of Mary Pinkney and two post-chaises for the chief mourners, heading for St Cuthbert's parish church in Darlington.

Sepr 17 a blustering Wind. Mama & I made a visit to Mrs Chapman.

Sepr 18 Tolerable day, some Showers of rain. Matty Beauly drank tea with us. Old Richard Burrell buried.

Thursday 19 fine day, my Sister badly in a Cold, we sat in Mama's Room all day. Mr Allen call'd.

19 September 1765

Now it is the Sister's turn to be unwell. William Allen is still home from London.

Friday 20 Mama very bad in the Gravel, in the Evening Mrs Wilson and Alice Nichols came in.

20 September 1765

'Gravel' was the name given to the painful condition of kidney stones, an accumulation of crystals which had to pass out of the urinary tract. The Diarist is about to go down with her sister's cold.

Sepr 21 Mama and Sister something better, got Cold my self. Some Showers of rain. In the Eve Mrs Wilson.

Sunday 22 Wet Morn, nobody at Church.

22 September 1765

None of the household felt well enough to brave the wet morning and attend church.

Monday 23 Wind with some Showers of rain, Mr Allen half an hour.

Sepr 24 (The Beast Fair) very fine day, in the Garden an hour. Drank Tea with Mrs Newsam, in the Eve A Nichols.

Fairday, 25 Fine day, I walk'd down Street into the Fair with Mrs Newsam, came home to tea.

25 September 1765

The annual two-day Rood Fair again merits mention, and the Diarist goes to see the stalls with her friend the grocer's wife.

Sepr 26 fine day, in the Garden an hour. After dinner I went to the danceing School along with Mrs Wilson. She came home with me and drank tea.

26 September 1765

Another Thursday performance from the dancing school.

Friday 27 fine day, at Prayers in the Morn. After dinner I sat an hour with Mrs Simpson, my Sister got a letter from Miss Mawer. I had a letter from Miss F. Emerson with some fruits. Mrs Wilson came in.

27 September 1765

A servant from Winston had brought the Diarist a letter from Fanny Emerson. Also some fruit from the rectory orchard, and her sister a letter from Bridget Mawer at nearby Gainford.

Saturday 28 Rainey Morn, I paid Mr Watson 8s. for a Tupee. Mr Knight gave us a call. In the Eve we had Miss Carr.

28 September 1765

A tupee was a raised roll of hair over which the owner's natural hair was combed forward to form a topknot.

Sunday 29 fine day, at Church Morn and Eve. I made a visit to Mrs Bowes.

29 September 1765

The feast day of St Michael and All Angels warranted attendance at church twice. 'Michaelmas' was a quarter day, when rents were paid and bills settled. The Diarist makes a thoughtful visit to the recently widowed Sally Bowes, left with two small children.

Monday 30 Wind and rain, saw nobody. Writeing to Winston.

<u>30 September 1765</u>

A rare day without any social engagements.

Octr 1 Shower of rain. In the Eve Mrs Wilson came in.

Wednesday 2 rain and wind. Betty washing.

Thursday 3 Blustering wind, in the Morn at Mrs Dixon's Shop, bought my Self a black hand[kerchief] 5s. After dinner Mrs Wilson and I went to the danceing School, got home to tea. He has got a fine School, 43 Scholars. Mr Wilson sat the Evening.

<u>3 October 1765</u>

The 'he' in the sentence seems to relate to the dancing master, whose tally of forty-three scholars is probably much greater than the number of pupils at the Wilsons' girls' school.

Friday 4 Claping [sic] and drying small Cloths. Mrs Wilson drank Tea with us. Some Showers of rain.

<u>4 October 1765</u>

The dialect word 'claping' is here used to describe smoothing laundered articles with the hands rather than an iron.

Octr 5 Ironing in the Morn. After dinner Mr Allen sat an hour. Rainey night. I went to bed at 8 o'clock very bad in a sore throat and pain in my head.

Sunday 6 Very badly in my Cold. Miss Carr drank tea with us. Violent rain.

Octr 7 Stormey day, Wind and rain. Badly all day, in the Eve Mrs Wilson sat an hour with us.

Tuesday 8 better in my Cold, Wind and rain.

Octr 9 Wind and rain, in the Afternoon Mr Allen sat an hour with us. Readheads has got a Family to bo[a]rd, their names Townsend.

9 October 1765

The Readheads, the Diarist's landlords, having a new family in their lodgings may be connected with the Mawers having moved to Gainford.

Thursday 10 The Sessions and Mayor's Feast. There is a prosecution against Miss Wrather's for having a Lottery. In the Eve Mrs Wilson came in. Wind and rain. Mr Wilson has got a new Border from Newcastle, her name Clark.

10 October 1765

The 'Sessions' were the Borough Quarter Sessions, held three-monthly, with the mayor of the day as chief magistrate. Poor Miss Wrather had come a legal cropper by holding a lottery without proper authorisation. Perhaps she was trying to emulate Faith Dixon who had had a fundraising raffle the previous October. Thomas Cornforth's mayoral feast was not a social event that the Diarist could attend, but an important function in the later part of his year of office, when he entertained the corporation. Again the Wilsons have recruited a pupil from Newcastle.

Friday 11 The same weather. Mr and Mrs Wilson drank tea.

Octr 12 After dinner Mr Allen came in. In the Eve Mrs Wilson and Alice Nichols.

12 October 1765

London residents William Allen and Alice Nicholls are still in Richmond.

Sunday 13 at Church Morn and Eve. Cold wind but no rain. Mama and I drank tea at Mrs Wilson's.

13 October 1765

Presumably Mama accompanied the Diarist to the two church services.

Monday 14 Cold wind, down Street, paid Mrs F. Dixon a bill of 2L. 12s. Drank tea there, wet night.

14 October 1765

The haberdashery credit account seems to be settled every six months.

Octr 15 Cold day. After dinner I sat an hour at Mr Wilson's, they came in and drank tea with us.

Octr 16 not very well, sat in Mama's Room all day.

16 October 1765

This seems to be only a brief indisposition.

Thursday 17 Violent wind. I sent a letter to Miss F. Emerson, in the Eve Mrs Wilson came in.

Friday 18 Ironing in the Morn, Miss Carr drank Tea with us.

Octr 19 Fine warm day. I walked down Street to Mrs Dixon's.

Sunday 20 Fine day. At Church Morn, and Eve. Mr Wilson drank Tea with us, in the Eve Mr Allen call'd, he go[e]s for London tomorrow Morn. My Sister sent a letter by him to Nanny Smith.

20 October 1765

William Allen, returning to duties in London, usefully saves postage by taking a letter, written by Sister, the household scribe, to their sister-in-law.

Octr 21 Fine, warm day, in the Garden an hour. After dinner I walk'd down to Matty's, drank Tea there, rainey Night.

Octr 22 Rainey Morn, I received a letter from Miss Fanny Emerson, and a basket of Pears. Mrs Strickland and the two young Ladies drank Tea with us, in the Eve Mrs Wilson came in.

22 October 1765

The Winston garden is still contributing to the Diarist's diet, and the pears came with a non-posted reply to the letter written to Fanny Emerson five days before. It would seem that Catherine Strickland was educating her youngest daughters Barbara and Charlotte in the etiquette of tea drinking.

Octr 23 Fine day, in the Garden an hour, Drank Tea at Mr Medcalf's. A. Nichols sat the Afternoon with Mama and Sister.

23 October 1765

The entry unusually specifies that Mama and Sister were both in the house together when the Diarist unfortunately missed Alice Nicholls's visit by being out.

Thursday 24 Fine day. I went to the Dancing School with Mrs Newsam and Mrs Medcalf, drank Tea at Mrs Newsam's.

24 October 1765

Another Thursday visit to the dancing school.

Friday 25 Fine day in the Garden in the Morn. After dinner Mrs Wilson and I walk'd to Ask[e] Wood. Mr and Mrs Wilson drank Tea with us.

25 October 1765

On a fine day the autumnal colours of the leaves in Aske Wood were doubtless well worth a longish walk to enjoy.

Saturday 26 Wet Morn. I drank Tea at Mr Wilson's.

Sunday 27 At Church Morn and Eve. Mr and Mrs Newsam drank Tea with us. Showers of rain.

27 October 1765

James Newsham could join in the tea-drinking, it being a Sunday when his shop was closed.

Monday 28 Cold day, in the Eve Mrs Wilson came in.

Octr 29 very Cold, A. Nichols sat the Eve with us.

Oct 30 Cold Showers of rain, Miss Carr drank Tea with us.

30 October 1765

Miss Carr, a favourite pupil from the Wilsons' school, frequently takes tea with the Diarist.

Octr 31 Miss Carr drank Tea with us, Mrs Wilson in ye Eve.

Novr 1 Wind and rain. After dinner I went into Mr Wilson's to ask them to drink Tea, they sat the Eve.

1 November 1765

The Diarist again gives us rare details of how the Georgians invited their friends to take tea.

Novr 2 Writeing to Winston. After dinner I went down Street to get some od[d] things, call'd upon Mrs Simpson, drank Tea at Mrs Dixon's, rainey Night.

2 November 1765

As it was Saturday market day, perhaps there was a carrier visiting from Teesdale who could deliver the letter to Winston cheaper than the postage. The Diarist must have spent most of the day out, shopping, calling on Mrs Simpson and then drinking tea with Faith Dixon.

Sunday 3 at Church in the Morn, Violent rain. Miss Carr drank Tea with us. Mrs Wilson in the Eve.

3 November 1765

As it was such an unpleasant day, visitors were from close by in other parts of Bowes Hall, Mrs Wilson and her pupil, Miss Carr.

Monday 4 Wind and rain. Mr and Mrs Wilson drank Tea.

Novr 5 Extreamly Cold, in the Morn a Shower of Snow, this day's Post brought the news of the death of his Royal Highness William Duke of Cumberland, he died last Thursday the 31 of Octr suddenly in his Chair.

5 November 1765

As none of the Diarist's London friends had recently arrived in Richmond, news of this national event took some days to reach the town, by official means. 'Butcher' Cumberland was highly regarded by local Whig supporters for having defeated the Jacobites. John Yorke had built a folly in his landscaped garden to commemorate the Hanoverian victory at the Battle of Culloden of 1746. Originally called Cumberland Temple, it is now known as Culloden Tower.

Novr 6 In the Morning a Shower of Snow. Mama and I drank Tea at Mrs Wilson's.

6 November 1765

The Diarist's elderly mother was able to enjoy some company by taking Tea in another part of the large building where they lived without going outside in the snowy conditions.

Novr 7 Fine Cold day. Mr Jackson brought home my Stays, I paid him 1L. 5s. 0d. He brought his Fiddle and play'd us two or three tunes. Mrs Wilson and A. Nichols came in.

7 November 1765

The Diarist had ordered her pair of stays on 9 August, so it had taken Robert Jackson two months to make them, hence the high cost of 25s. He lived in Frenchgate, quite near the Diarist. He was known to be a good violinist.

Friday 8 This day orders came for General Mourning for his late Royal Highness the Duke of Cumberland to begin on Sunday next. I drank Tea at Mr Wilson's. I went with Mrs Wilson and her Young Ladies to the Dancing School, it being a Publick Night, we stay'd tel 10 o'clock. A Child buried with the Small Pox.

8 November 1765

The dancing school was fortunate in being able to continue with its public performance as the general mourning for the king's brother was to begin two days later. John Cowling's son William, having died of smallpox, would be a cause of anxiety for everyone, particularly the young ladies at the Wilsons' school. His death would seem have been the first of a nasty outbreak of the disease.

Novr 9 Busy preparing for mourning. Miss Carr drank tea.

9 November 1765

The official period of mourning for a senior member of the royal family required preparations. Social events had to be cancelled as well as sombre clothes prepared.

Novr 10 Wet Morn, at Church Morn and Eve. Mr and Mrs Wilson drank Tea with us.

Monday 11 Fine day, Mr and Mrs Hutchinson drank Tea with us. Old Frances Allen Buried.

11 November 1765

The parish register of burials also has this in what we regard as the feminine spelling, but it seems more likely that it was the very aged Mr Francis Allen who had died.

Tuesday 12 Mama badly in the Giddyness in her head, in the Eve Mrs Wilson came in. Rainey night.

Novr 13 Fine day, another Child of John Cowling Buried in the Small pox.

13 November 1765

This John Cowling, who had now lost his son Cuthbert to smallpox, only a few days after the death of another son William, was a shoemaker. The parish register entries included the occupations of the fathers when there were two families of the same name in the town.

Thursday 14 Fine day, Mrs Wilson came for half an hour. A. Nichols sat the Evening with us. Cast on Mama a pair of White Worsted Stockings.

14 November 1765

The Diarist is knitting her Mama some stockings. Worsted is a very fine woollen yarn. Georgian Richmond had a prosperous industry in the hand knitting, and exporting, of stockings using much coarser local wool. Stockings were worn with knee-length breeches by men, instead of modern socks.

Friday 15 Fine warm day.

Novr 16 Rain all day. I recvd a letter from Miss F. Emerson with some Apples and Pears. Mama very bad in her Back.

16 November 1765

The Winston rectory orchard has produced more apples and pears, presumably of varieties which kept into the winter. They and the letter would have been brought by a servant of the Emersons or a local carrier.

Sunday 17 Fine day, at Church Morn and Eve, I drank Tea at Mrs Euebanks, got a letter from Mrs Huggans.

Monday 18 Fine day, down Street at the Shops at Miss Wayd's, I got Mama a Silk Handkerchief 4s. 6d., my Self a pair of shoes, and a Pocket Han[kerchie]f 2s. 9d. At Mrs Dixon's I got my Self a yd and [?]half of plain gauze for an Apron 3s. 6d. a yd. Drank Tea at Mrs Newsam's, in the Eve Miss Mawer cal'd upon us.

18 November 1765

The Diarist was splashing out on items of apparel from two shops. Doubtless Bridget Mawer would admire the purchases when she called in the evening, she was obviously staying in Richmond for a day or two before returning to Gainford.

Novr 19 Fine day, in the Morn Miss Mawer cal'd, she is going home.

Novr 20 Frost. Betty washing, Mama badly.

21 Frost. Starching and drying Small Cloths, in the afternoon Dr. Pringle sat an hour with us.

21 November 1765

Dr Pringle, the Diarist's friend and doctor, seems not to have attended Mama, so the improvement in her health after his visit may be coincidence.

Friday 22 Frost. Ironing all day, Mama better.

22 November 1765

It would take a long time to iron starched cloths to the standard required for Tea without a modern steam iron.

Novr 23 Fine day. Betty Beautiment dined with us. A little Girl of Mr Hutchinson's at the Hill buried at Catterick.

23 November 1765

Poor little Lucy Hutchinson of Hill House was buried at Catterick only about fifteen weeks after her mother Martha on 14 August.

Novr 24 at Church Morn and Eve, Mr and Mrs Wilson drank Tea with us. Cuthbert Sadler buried.

24 November 1765

Richard Sadler's son Cuthbert seems to have died from some cause other than smallpox.

Monday 25 Fine day.

Novr 26 Rain all day.

Novr 27 Fine day, I drank tea at Mr Wilson's.

Thursday 28 Very fine day, in the Garden half an hour, we got a new Almanack, cost 9d. Old Jane Clarkson buried.

28 November 1765

A 'very fine day' is certainly worthy of comment in late November. The price of this new almanac, 9d being possibly about £6 in 2016 terms, suggests it must have been far superior to those of an average price. The Diarist was away from home this time last year, so we don't know if she bought one then, and if so what it cost, but it was an essential aid for a thoroughly modern Diarist.

Friday 29 Fine day. Mrs Wilson sat the Eve with us.

Novr 30 Frost. Mama wrote to Mr Robinson to B[arnard] Cas[tle] for Candles and Sent 16s. for the last Candles.

30 November 1765

It seems strange that Mama sent for candles from Barnard Castle, when presumably they were available in Richmond, but there may have been a family connection.

Decr 1 dark day, badly in me head, I drank tea at Mr Wilson's.

1 December 1765

The phrase 'in me head' would pass as Yorkshire dialect even today.

Decr 2 dark day, Mrs Medcalf drank Tea with us. A Child of Sergeant Cambles buried in ye Small Pox.

2 December 1765

The latest victim of the outbreak of smallpox to be mentioned was the daughter of Alexander Campbell, a sergeant in the North York Militia. According to the parish register she had the intriguing name Gerada. The word 'Cambles' is a good example of the Diarist writing phonetically the name 'Campbell's'. She has also used the modern spelling 'sergeant', whereas the Georgian spelling was usually 'serjeant', the form still used in Richmond today for the two civic posts of senior and junior 'serjeant at mace'.

Tuesday 3 Mama very bad in the pain in her Back. I drink Tea at Mrs Colingwood's.

Wednesday 4 very Cold day, thick fog, Mr and Mrs Wilson drank tea.

Thursday 5 Slight frost, very badly all day.

Friday 6 Thick Fog all day, in the Eve a Violent Shower of rain.

6 December 1765

The fine spell of autumn weather has quickly turned into winter.

Dec 7 Recvd by John Todd 5L. on Matthew Graham's account. I wrote a letter to Miss F. E(merson), did not get it sent.

7 December 1765

This £5 is virtually the only income recorded by the Diarist. Its source may have been Thomas Smith, or possibly the Emersons. 'Mr Mathew Graham of Richmond, gentleman, formerly of Easby Parish, aged 86' was buried at Easby on 3 March 1805, so he must have had links with the area. His name occurs four times in the diary, but always from elsewhere as communications to and from him are by letter, or an intermediary, as in this case. The Diarist's sister had written to him in Ireland in June.

Sunday 8 Cold day, at Church Morn and Evening, drank Tea at Mr Wilson's.

Monday 9 We had a Card from Miss Mawer with a bottle of Syrup of Cloves from Mrs Mawer, a present to Mama. I drank Tea at Mrs Colingham's I got 6 p[oun]d of Lint at Masterman's, the quakers 14d. pd.

9 December 1765

One must hope the syrup of cloves alleviated Mama's various complaints. James Masterman, the Quaker grocer, later moved to Stockton-on-Tees. Presumably the 'lint' was linen fibre that the Diarist began spinning, though it is unclear why it was bought from a grocer. Spinning would take up part of nine days out of the next twelve.

Decr 10 Rain, Mr and Mrs Wilson drank tea with us. A. Nichols spent the Eve. This Morn I began to Spin.

Decr 11 Rain, Spinning in the morning.

Thursday 12 Frost very Cold, Spinning in the Morn. After dinner I went with Mrs Wilson to the Dancing School, she came home with me and drank tea.

12 December 1765

The last attendance at the dancing school mentioned in the diary.

Friday 13 Frost, Spinning in the Morn, drank tea at Mr Wilson's. Widow Robinson's little boy buried in the Small pox.

13 December 1765

Smallpox, first mentioned five weeks earlier, is about to become prevalent among the children of the town. The parish register records the burial of John, son of Mary Robinson.

Decr 14 hard frost, my Sister got a letter from Miss F. Emerson, return'd an answer. Spinning all day.

14 December 1765

Presumably the Diarist's letter to Fanny Emerson, begun on 7 December, had eventually been sent.

Sunday 15 hard frost, at Church in the Eve. Miss Carr, Miss Clark, Miss Gambles and Miss Foss from Mrs Wilson's drank tea with us, we received two letters, one from Nanny Smith & one from Mina.

15 December 1765

This is one of the larger gatherings of the Wilsons' boarders, presumably some local pupils went home at the weekends, leaving these from further away at rather a loss on a chilly wintry day. Again there is mention of letters being received on a Sunday, the second one is probably from Wilhelmina, the Diarist's niece in London.

Monday 16 Hard frost, Mr and Mrs Wilson drank tea with us. A. Nichols spent the Eve with us.

Decr 17 Fine day, not frost, Spinning all day.

Wednesday 18 Fine day, Spinning in the Morn. Mrs Wilson and A. Nichols sat an hour with us in the Evening. A Child Buried in the Small pox, this is the 5th.

18 December 1765

Alice Nicholls will be returning to London at the end of the month. The evening conversation has included adding up the recent smallpox deaths.

Decr 19 Fine day, Spinning in the Morn. Cap'n Moor call'd and drank tea with us, in the Eve Mrs Wilson came in, a Child buried.

19 December 1765

Captain Moor, who also visited in August, was related to the Revd Moor of Teesdale.

Friday 20 Fine day, Spinning, my Sister wrote to Nanny Smith by Mr Stoupe.

20 December 1765

The Diarist's sister was replying to a letter from Nanny Smith received the previous Sunday. Revd John Stoupe, the bachelor Perpetual Curate of Trinity chapel in Richmond market place, was presumably going to London, perhaps to spend Christmas with his family.

Decr 21 Cold rain, got a letter from Mr Robinson with 3 doz. of Candles 19s. A Child of Mr Renoldson's buried in the Small pox, this is the 6th.

21 December 1765

The candles Mama ordered three weeks earlier have arrived.

Sunday 22 Cold day, in the Eve a Covering of Snow, at Church Morn and Eve, Mr and Mrs Wilson drank tea with us.

Decr 23 Cold day, my Uncle Emerson's Man call'd and brought us some apples, he came for Dr. Pringle for Mrs Holms. Miss Carr brought me a Ticket for the Ball, she drank tea with us.

23 December 1765

Revd John Emerson had a male employee who could be sent over from Winston to Richmond on errands. In this case, bringing the Diarist apples from the rectory orchard for her Christmas fare, as well as asking for Dr Pringle to travel out to see Mrs Holmes, a relative of his curate, Revd Thomas Holmes Tidy. This indicates again how highly Richmond medical practitioners were regarded. Miss Carr, the pupil of the Wilsons most highly favoured by the Diarist, had brought her a ticket for the dancing school ball the following week, perhaps as a thank you for all the tea she had shared!

Christmas Eve Frost, at prayers in the Morn, from thence to Mrs Dixon's, got Mama 3 pocket hand[kerchie]ves. Butter 11d. a pd.

24 December 1765

Last-minute Christmas shopping is apparently nothing new! The price of butter, which was more expensive at Christmas time, has caused comment.

Christmas Day very fine day, at Church the Morn and Eve. A. Nichols drank tea and spent the Eve with us. Dr. Pringle sat half an hour with us. 2 funerals, William Crowder junior & a Child in the Small pox ye 7th.

25 December 1765

The Christmas Day church services probably included one of the four annual celebrations of Holy Communion. There is no reference to the Roman Catholic Dr Pringle's attendance at a Catholic service. It seems strange now that two burials in Richmond churchyard actually took place on Christmas Day.

Thursday 26 Fine day. Miss Carr drank tea with us, a young Woman Buried.

26 December 1765

This was a working day, not a public holiday as later.

Friday 27 Frost, fine day at Prayers in the Morn, Mr and Mrs Wilson drank tea and spent the Eve with us.

Decr 28 Frost, paid Betty Beautyment for Butter 7s. 6d. Miss Carr drank tea with us.

Betty Beautyment was in Richmond at the Saturday market, and had supplied many pounds of butter over a period of several weeks before the bill was settled.

Sunday 29 Frost, very Cold, I drank tea at Mrs Wilson's. Nelly King Buried. Alice Nichols went to York in her way to London.

The travel arrangements of Alice Nicholls are interesting. Why did she travel as far as York to catch a London coach? Why not go from Catterick Bridge? Perhaps she had other business to attend to in York. It would also seem unusual for the era that she travelled on a Sunday.

Monday 30 Frost, the Dancing School Ball. I went in the Chaise with Miss Carr and Miss Foss. A Child buried in the Small pox the 8th.

A rare treat for the Diarist to ride in a hired chaise with two of the Wilsons' boarders to the dancing school ball, for which Miss Carr had sent her a ticket.

Decr 31 Frost, Miss Carr drank tea and Spent ye Eve.

Did they extravagantly keep the candles burning while they sat up and saw in the New Year?

New Year's Day Mr Mrs Wilson and Miss Carr drank tea with us.

The calendar year had only changed on 1 January since 1753; the new year previously had started each 25 March, hence the Diarist's up-to-date usage, and the need to set out the date fully with the new year in the following entry. Miss Carr spends the

whole of the Christmas and New Year period at the Wilsons' school,
without returning to Newcastle.

Jan 2 1766 Hard frost, Mrs Chapman drank tea with us.

Friday 3 Frost and a Covering of Snow. Spinning in the Morn, drank tea at Mr Wilson's, Mama badly in a cold.

Jan 4 Frost and Snow. Miss Carr drank Tea with us.

Sunday 5 Frost and Snow. Orders for a General Mourning to begin this day, for his late Royal Highness Frederick William, the King's youngest Brother, His Highness died last Sunday. Mrs Crowder buried, in the Eve I sat an hour at Mr Wilson's.

5 January 1766

Another period of national mourning for a member of the royal family begins. The death of Mrs Crowder occurs only a few days after that of her son William.

Jan 6 1766 Frost. Spinning in the Morn. Mr & Mrs Wilson drank tea with us. Mama badly in a Cold.

Tuesday 7 Frost. Spinning in the Morn, saw nobody.

Wednesday 8 Frost. Spinning in the Morning. Miss Carr drank tea with us. Mama better in her Cold.

8 January 1766

As Mama is elderly and not in good health generally, she has done well to throw off her winter cold so quickly.

Jan. ye 9th Frost, down Street at Mrs Dixon's Shop, got my Self a Check'd Apron cost 9d. Call'd at Mrs Newsam's, came home to tea.

9 January 1766

The small price of the checked apron suggests that it was a practical rather than a decorative garment.

Friday 10 Hard frost, Miss Carr drank tea with us.

Saturday 11 Frost. I wrote to Mrs Huggans at Ampleford, sat an hour at Mr Wilson's.

11 January 1766

The Diarist's link with Mrs Huggans is unexplained. Contact was always by letter. She seems to have had some link with Francis Allen. This fourth entry locates her at 'Ampleford', which may be Ampleforth near Helmsley.

Sunday 12 hard frost, at Church Morn and Evening, drank tea and Supd at Mr Wilson's. A Child of John Maxwell's buried.

12 January 1766

The supper taken at Mr Wilson's is a rare example of the Diarist eating at someone else's house. John Maxwell was a peruke-maker who had premises in the Toll Booth, the large Georgian commercial building which stood in Richmond market place.

Monday 13 hard frost, spinning in the Morn, after dinner I walk'd down Street, drank tea at Mrs Simpson's. Mr Caleb Readshaw chose Mayor. A Child buried in the Small pox, this is the 9th. Mrs Wilson supd.

13 January 1766

Caleb Readshaw had only become an alderman the previous year, so he had not been elected mayor on seniority. His sister Jane would later marry Thomas Cornforth, Readshaw's predecessor as mayor.

Tuesday 14 hard frost, I wrote to my Uncle Smith by Mama's order and sent the two sertificates. Mrs Temple buried. I drank tea at Mr Wilson's.

14 January 1766

The two certificates required by Thomas Smith remain a mystery, but it sounds as though they were important, either to him, to Mama, or to the Diarist. Sarah Temple was the wife of Anthony Temple, master of Richmond Grammar School from 1750 to 1796. Early in their marriage she suffered a stroke and was paralysed. He used to carry her in his arms to church.

Jan 15 Frost. Spinning in the Morn. Betty washing.

15 January 1766

The penultimate entry of the diary shows a day given over to practical tasks, with no social activity.

Jan 16 Frost, Mr and Mrs Wilson drank tea and spent the Evening with us.

16 January 1766

> *The final diary entry ends it on a typical note, the frosty weather which had continued since Christmas, and the time spent with the Wilsons, the couple the Diarist had spent most time with since the departure of the Mawers.*

Postscript

No sooner had the writing of *Life in Georgian Richmond* been completed and the proofs corrected than, most unexpectedly, the will of Frances Robson – argued in the book to have been the Diarist – turned up.

Given what had emerged from the evidence assembled concerning the Smith family, it is not surprising that the principal bequests are to her nephew and nieces, the children of her brother, Layton Smith – Layton, Ann and Wilhelmina. So that would seem to confirm that the Diarist was Frances Robson: the 'Diary and its Secrets' had indeed given up its principal secret.

Yet what is surprising in the will are the quantities and qualities of furniture and tableware specified. Of course one expects the 'set of best Tea China', but what about all the silverware, including the 'Silver Coffee Pot and Stand', the 'Silver cream Jugg' and especially 'one Dozen of silver Tea spoons, Mark'd with the Crest'? Of course all of these, and the items of furniture, could have belonged to Frances' deceased husband. But if not, then we are sent back to that subtitle, 'The Diary and its Secrets'.

BW

Sources of Information

Life in Georgian Richmond, North Yorkshire has drawn on numerous original sources in addition to 'The Richmond Diary' itself. Many of these are in the North Yorkshire County Record Office at Northallerton (NYCRO), including the relevant parish registers for Richmond (NYCRO PR/RM 1/5) and Easby (NYCRO PR/ EAS 1/2), the Richmond deeds in the Dundas/Zetland archive (NYCRO I 1/1-2643) and Richmond Corporation Leases (NYCRO DC/RMB 5 1/1-847). Transcriptions of some of these, and others, were among the archives left by L. P. Wenham, which have also been heavily used, as has his invaluable record of the inscriptions on the tombstones in Richmond churchyard. Several volumes in the NYCRO Publications series have also been of considerable assistance, as have publications of the Cleveland Family History Society.

The wills of Thomas Smith and William Cornforth were transcribed from copies held by the National Archives. Andrew Mussell of Gray's Inn, Clare Owen of Raby Castle and Keith Sweetmore, formerly of NYCRO, have helpfully provided answers to queries. Dr Rachel Greenwood of NYCRO kindly gave us an analysis of the manuscript itself. Professor Ian Beckett and Professor Stephen Conway gave advice on military movements. Various online resources have been used, particularly concerning William and Layton Smith, and also the Clergy of the Church of England database. Considerable use has been made of the Bill Bryson and Palace Green libraries of the University of Durham.

The authors are extremely grateful to their good friend, graphic designer Andy Thursfield, for his advice and help with the illustrations. Many friends have generously shared their professional expertise, including Gordon Alexander, Stella Birch, Adrian Bullock (Associate Lecturer and Consultant, Oxford International Centre for Publishing Studies), Jules Dann, Prebendary Jacqueline Fox, Richard Green, Val Hepworth, Dr Frank Heron, Dr Julian Litten, Marion Moverley, Danielle Triggs (West Yorkshire Archive Service), Steve Wade and Ralph Waggett. Sir Alfred Edward Pease's *A Dictionary of the Dialect of the North Riding of Yorkshire* (1928) has also been useful. Grateful thanks to all at Pen and Sword Ltd, and especially to Claire Hopkins, Karyn Burnham and Janet Brookes.

Index